# Ancestral River

A Spiritual Journey for the Living and the Dead

Carla Adams

For more information, email carla.m@ancestralriver.com

ISBN: 979-8-88759-866-6 - paperback

ISBN: 979-8-88759-867-3 - ebook

ISBN: 979-8-89109-159-7 - hardcover

## Get Your Free Gift!

Begin your own ancestral river journey by listening to this free biofield sound therapy session, *Clearing Your Future, Clearing Your Past*.

Worry about the future and regretting—or dwelling on—past mistakes and traumas are common unhelpful thought patterns often shared by our ancestors. This biofield session helps clear those patterns, increase your attention to the present moment, and create a feeling of ease in your mind.

With your mind in the present moment, you will be better able to listen to your intuition, so this session tunes your pineal gland, the center of your sense of intuition. This session also tunes your heart chakra to allow greater love for self and generations past and future, and tunes your root chakra to increase your awareness of the safety and abundance that all generations share with the universe. In addition, it tunes your foot chakras to help you take your next steps forward in your journey to freedom from unhelpful thought patterns for you, your ancestors, and your descendents.

**Clearing Your Future, Clearing Your Past**

Download your free copy by visiting:

https://www.ancestralriver.com/free-session

With many thanks to our wonderful universe,
to my husband, for his constant love and support, and
to the friends who encouraged me in my journey.

With special thanks to Stacy, who made this book possible,
to Dr. Sue Morter, for inspiring me to listen to my spirit,
and to Kim Woods and Team, for helping me discover
the power of the universe within me.

# Table of Contents

# Introduction

My life journey was full of difficulties; lack of self-love and feelings of unworthiness were the lens through which I viewed life. Three years of practicing meditation, connecting with nature, giving and receiving energy healing modalities, and using self-help exercises every day changed the lens.

This book is the story of my personal growth, spiritual awakening, and the wisdom and knowledge I received from divine sources during three-and-a-half years, woven together in chronological order.

I found that our journey doesn't end at death. By experiencing the continued relationship I have with my ancestors after their deaths, I gained an understanding of the interconnectedness of everything in the universe and my value as an integral part of the whole. I hope my story will help readers know their value also, and encourage them to fully express their own desires for the highest good of all.

In Resources, I have provided links to many of the people I have learned from, and to illustrations of ideas presented in the book.

# Chapter 1

# My Dream

Drenched and chilled, my husband and I placed buckets to catch roof runoff and dumped the full ones into large shipping totes to keep the building site from being swamped. It was our fifth day in the tarp shack; twenty-six inches fell in our first three weeks.

Three of our five acres were already cleared of trees, but we moved rocks and leveled dirt to add a living area and a greenhouse to the tarp shack. My husband erected stud walls using a gas generator for power tools, while I planted a garden and orchard into rocky ground.

We were surrounded by nature. A picnic cooler served as our refrigerator, a single-burner propane stove cooked food and heated water, and a foil-covered cardboard box topped with glass baked cake or bread on sunny days. The camping toilet and shower bag were half-hidden behind a row of scraggly trees. Bug repellant, salve for fire ant bites, a flashlight, and bear spray were always within reach.

Making a trip to bring the rest of our belongings to our homestead, we drove at dusk to escape the heat. Our repurposed school bus, dash lights flashing, slowed to a crawl on the interstate. We spent the night in a parking lot.

The mechanic said, "Parts and labor will cost at least $3,500."

We had already discussed a worst-case scenario. "That's twice what we paid for it; what could we get as scrap?"

We parked a rental truck at my in-laws', where we had lived the past four years while helping care for my husband's aging father, loaded up, and drove nine hours back to our homestead.

Buying the old bus for our move, plus needing to rent this truck, took much of our savings. And now we need to buy another vehicle. As if hearing my thoughts, my husband said, "Don't let me buy another bus."

I turned toward the window but couldn't see through tears. "I'd probably kill you."

Pain, fever, vomiting, and diarrhea lasted days; I slept through most of two weeks, except to find medicinal herbs to dull the pain. As the weather turned cooler, I pulled on a pair of old jeans; they fell to the floor. Cinching them with a rope, I began to putter in the garden, too weak to work.

Without the bus, we needed a four-wheel drive to make it to town in winter, but even old trucks in poor condition were expensive. My older son found us one we could pay cash for;

we left our car with him, hoping it would sell to recoup the price of the truck.

He called a few days later. "Does your car leak? A guy came for a test drive; it rained last night and the floors are soaked."

No! We don't need this now. I sighed. "We didn't know. Bumping around on the trail to our place must have broken a seal."

One day, my husband said, "We won't finish the house and fireplace before winter. We can stay with my folks again to save some money."

"I think I can get most of my cleaning and gardening jobs back again. Let's move before it gets too cold."

A week later, my husband was under the truck, cussing. "The new part doesn't fit, and I had to cut out the rusted piece. We can't drive the truck!"

I called the only person in town we knew. "Our only vehicle broke down; we ordered a part that will be delivered to the post office. We have a post office box, but can the rural driver leave the package at the end of our road?"

The postmaster said, "No problem."

Temperatures dropped low. I called the postmaster again. "The truck part got lost during shipping. If we find another part at a local store or salvage yard, is there anyone in town we can hire to drive us there?"

"I'll take off work tomorrow and drive you wherever you need to go. How do I get to your place?"

"Our trail's in bad shape; we'll meet you at the blacktop by the neighbor's mailbox."

Walking two miles in coveralls carrying my laptop, we arrived just as she did. We bought a few groceries and an extra five gallons of propane for heat, then used the internet at the convenience store to search for the truck part. We had to order again.

Returning home late afternoon, I opened the gate for the postmaster to drive through; bright fall colors flashed from the hills, surrounding the little house at the back of the clearing. She said, "It's so beautiful; I can see why you live here."

We waited ten days of overcast skies, wearing long underwear and insulated coveralls, sitting near the single-burner stove shivering. With nights below freezing, we warmed bricks, wrapped them in towels, and placed them at the foot of the air mattress. Layers of blankets under and over us, we stayed warm from early dusk to long past dawn.

My husband installed the part a few hours after we got it. We loaded the truck and left. Four months of income and a warm house renewed our enthusiasm for our dream, and we were back at the first sign of spring, with the pickup and our small car.

The house, garden, and a second greenhouse progressed for a few weeks, but everything cost more and took longer than planned. I said, "One of us will have to look for work."

Both our vehicles were old; it would be a long drive every day. My husband said, "I don't want you stuck in the dark on the hairpin curve. I'll get a job."

The first day my husband left for work, sunrise was beautiful. Birds sang as I tended the garden, making it feel like a nest surrounded by trees. Looking at the garden from the afternoon shade, my gaze swept over the melons, flowers, herbs, and orchard spread before me. My dream has come true!

The first week went quickly with chores and projects. I glanced at the calendar. Saturday; I bet there's a garage sale in town! But the trail will tear up the car, and I shouldn't drive it more than we have to. There's no extra money anyways.

With summer heat and no rain, we hauled in water twice a week. I waited to make the trip in the evening when my husband was home to share the work of unloading the five-gallon bottles that filled the bed of the truck. It was a date night—we stopped for cold drinks.

I sat in the shade watching the thermometer top one hundred degrees. It was in the shade too. I loved growing up on a farm. My husband and I lived in the country before, and we loved it. But, I always had family, school, or work. I need people.

When my husband got home, I said, "How about I ride to town with you once a week to do laundry and get groceries?"

In the truck-stop dining room at seven the next morning, I was still alone, but air conditioning felt wonderful. The laundromat and grocery store had air conditioning too. But every store had different people every week; I stumbled over words. I'm so used to being by myself that I can't carry a conversation.

Ouch! I slapped the fire ant bite so hard it hurt. I hate these ants! As I pushed the mower over rocky ground to keep weeds from taking over, it hit a rock and stalled. I hate mowing! If living here is my dream, why don't I love it? I miss my boys! Both have been on their own for years, but I need them! I haven't seen them for months. I've always been able to travel. Now, I never have enough money to visit them. I threw the rock into the trees and started the mower. I need to see my boys.

Too antsy to stay home by myself all the time, I hauled in water, spraying myself from the fill-up hose to cool off. These bottles are too heavy! And I didn't have a date night.

Even in the heat, weeds flourished. Memories circled with the mower, tears streaking the dust on my face. Why did they blame me? What happened to my mind? I hate myself for getting fired. I shouldn't have sold everything when we moved. My in-laws were really nice, but living with them was so limiting. I have never fully grieved. Dad, I miss you so much!

I snapped at my husband. "We'll never get the fireplace built before winter at this rate. I refuse to be that cold again!"

"There's still time."

"The greenhouse isn't getting done. How will we afford to eat if we can't grow most of our food?"

"What do you expect? I'm working all the time!"

"We don't have enough money to build the fireplace."

"I'm doing all I can. I don't have time for this!"

Pulling the water wagon up to the orchard, I struggled to hold back tears. I've felt sad and lonely so much of my life. I can't shake it off this time. I need to see my boys again. I miss them so much.

I passed the peach tree and two raspberries plants that had died last week, stopped at an apple tree, and poured a bucket of water around the base of the tree. The leaves were turning brown. It wasn't going to make it.

Tears dropped on the dirt. I don't know if I'll make it.

I'd waited to be an adult, thinking I'd feel happy, waited for marriage, thinking I'd feel loved, and waited for our life here. But I'm still sad. . . .

That evening I said, "Living here isn't working for me; I can't do it anymore. I have to do whatever it takes to feel better inside."

"I know. I'll move anywhere you think you'll be happy."

# Chapter 2

# Starting Over

I grabbed the phone; my older son lived halfway between our mothers. "Are you still thinking of buying a rental property? We'll rent it."

"Okay. What kind of house do you want?"

"The house doesn't matter, but we need half an acre with enough sunshine for a big garden."

I called my younger son to tell him the news. He said, "If you need money, I'll send you enough to cover all your moving expenses."

I hated being in debt, but it would take most of the money we had left to finish projects so our place could sell quickly. "We'll pay you back when it sells."

A real estate agent listed our land and rented us another moving van. We stayed with my mother-in-law again until my son found a rental. My husband got a job transfer, and I was welcomed back to house cleaning and gardening jobs.

Searching through self-help podcasts in every spare moment, I heard about balancing the masculine and feminine energies within me. Growing up, I'd reacted emotionally or did what I thought others expected of me. As a single mom for sixteen years, I had tried to live more like the men I worked with—practical and focused—while the past few years I had just worked hard and avoided feelings. My life and emotions were seldom balanced.

Our real estate agent called. "You have an offer; if all goes as planned, you'll get your money in six weeks."

My son called. "Hey, Mom, go online. Tell me what you think of this house."

It was on a half-acre lot in a tiny town and had three bedrooms, two baths, and two garages. "Perfect!"

One day, I waited at the door for my husband to come home from work. "Did you know the universe is electric and that our thoughts and emotions flow in a donut shape—a torus—in light waves around our bodies? It's called a biofield, and extends five or six feet away from our bodies. Emotions like fear and anger make the light particles get stuck within the light waves, and eventually the stuck energy causes negative thought patterns and physical illnesses."

"That makes sense."

"There's a type of sound therapy that uses tuning forks as biofeedback. The vibration of the sound waves intersects with the light waves; the mind feels where the flow is blocked and releases the stuck particles. It helps people feel better. I need this; I can heal myself and clear all the junk I passed down to my boys at the same time!"

I made a down payment to reserve my place in the tuning fork class.

My son called. "You can move next week."

The house had sheltered over a century of ancestors before us; it needed as much healing as I did. Antique furniture once used by my grandparents surrounded me again; I was home.

Our real estate agent called. "Your buyer is in jail; the contract may fall through."

I slammed the phone and stomped out the door. Why can't life be easy? I can't afford the tuning fork class if the house doesn't sell! I can't handle losing another dream! Life hurts too much. . . .

But if I end it all, I'll never see my boys again. I have to stop the pain.

When I entered the house an hour later, my husband said, "What do you think will happen with the property?"

My voice was as void of feeling as my heart. "I don't care. I really don't care."

He looked me in the eye, then looked away. "I don't know where you found this person, but I never want to see her again."

My eyes filled with tears. Our marriage has always been full of love and support; I want to keep it that way. The boys need my love too. A deep breath cleared my mind; their love was worth the pain.

Two weeks later, the title company called. "The buyer is short a couple thousand, but I'm sending your check today; the real estate agents will have to wait for their commission."

When the money arrived, I repaid my younger son for our moving expenses, ordered tuning forks, and scheduled the class. I looked forward to filling my life with sound again. For much of my life, I had played piano and organ in church services and often strummed an acoustic guitar to accompany my singing. But during the past several years, I had not attended church or played music. When my tuning forks arrived, I practiced with them every day to fill my body and biofield with their vibration.

I listened to recorded biofield sessions to begin clearing my old emotional patterns, and read books about how energy flowed in our bodies. I learned about the emotions and thought patterns each energy center—called chakras—held.

After I watched one online video, I said to my husband, "This program would really help us. It says our thoughts and intentions are really important, and that intentions held by a group of people have more power for change than just one person. They offer a Zoom group to meet with and lots of encouragement for twelve months."

He wanted to spend the rest of our check wisely. "Would you be able to continue your progress without it?"

"If we made sure we took time to be the support group for each other, I think so."

He was working a job he didn't like and using days off to make repairs to our house. "Join the class. I'll learn from it too."

Every day I wrote down the blessings and miracles I received and recorded changes in my thoughts and behaviors. I listened to guided meditations and learned to connect with God in a deeper way than I had before. Through Zoom, I met with other women to share intentions, support, and love.

In a few weeks, I traveled to the tuning fork class. During a practice session, a student's fork screeched at the edge of my biofield. An instructor looked toward the massage table where I was lying. "Do you know your birth story?"

"My brother was colicky and only seven months old when Mom became pregnant again. Mom told me she felt overwhelmed; she wanted more children, but not so soon."

"Class, send her love for an untimely pregnancy."

A few inches later, the forks found more stuck energy. The instructor said, "Do you remember what happened when you were seven?"

I spoke my first thought. "I wanted to learn to light the fire in the woodstove, but I was afraid and kept dropping the matches. Wanting to please Dad, I decided I would hold on to the next match no matter what. Dad turned away for a few seconds; my thumb was black."

Soon the student was stuck in another pocket of energy. The instructor said, "Now you're ten."

"I hated myself and my body; I felt fat and ugly."

"And what was going on when you were fourteen?"

"I had anorexia until I was nineteen. I had friends, but I felt that if they really knew me, they wouldn't like me. I wanted to feel like I really belonged. Starving and throwing up to lose weight became my focus; I didn't feel so out of control."

"Now you're twenty-five."

"My husband was a drug addict and alcoholic. Life was scary."

"Class, send her love for an abusive marriage."

I felt the fear dissolve, but more energy was ready to clear. The instructor asked, "Carla, what happened at twenty-eight?"

"He held a knife to my throat as I nursed my baby."

"And when you were thirty-one?"

"My second divorce. I felt I had ruined my life and the lives of my children."

I knew what the last pocket was before she asked. "My boys were having a rough year in junior high. I blamed myself."

As the last pocket of my stuck energy cleared and the session ended, I felt as if a weight had been lifted from me. The instructor placed her hands on my ankles to support me. Just then, a drum sounded from the next room. The instructor's eyes shined with intuition; the drumming was a sign from the universe. "Your pulse has the same beat as the drum—the beat of a victory march!"

# Chapter 3

# Grandpa

In the weeks following the class, I received sessions from a practitioner, as well as from another student. At class, I had learned that the universe responded to our thoughts and intentions, so I also tuned myself by using a hologram and holding the intention that I was lying on the massage table even though I was standing beside it working. I could feel all the stuck energy in my hologram as easily as I could while doing a session in person! I felt happier after every session; old patterns didn't trigger as often.

I signed up for free online classes to discover why the old patterns had formed and how I could change them. I learned that from conception to age seven or eight years old, the mind believes everything it's told; it keeps us safe by following a known pattern. But if a parent gets angry, a child can feel fear or sadness and think that whatever happened was their fault, that something must be wrong with them, or that they weren't worthy or good enough. If other situations cause the same thoughts to be repeated several times in the child's early years, the thoughts become patterns based on feelings, not on truth.

My thoughts had written sad stories: fear of rejection and the need for approval. As a child, I had often begged for forgiveness so I wouldn't go to hell. As a teenager, I had starved myself because I thought I was fat. What had happened to me to cause these patterns?

As I walked along a country road enjoying nature, I remembered the Bible story of Adam and Eve; they had a connection with God and were experiencing the great abundance of the universe. But they were new on earth; maybe they had formative minds like children. They had heard the lies of the serpent, "Go ahead, eat the fruit—God doesn't want you to have the wisdom and knowledge he has."

Perhaps Eve had reacted in fear. "Why doesn't God want me to have wisdom? Have I done something wrong? Or is he mad at me? Do I need to protect myself?"

Maybe the lie had been repeated until Eve believed her thoughts. "If God doesn't want me to have it, something must be wrong with me; maybe I'm not worthy of having it. I must not be good enough."

Moved to tears, I said to God, "I don't know if Eve or whoever she represents was real, but if that person exists in the spirit world, I want her to know I understand. She believed the lies because her mind was designed to protect her. It wasn't her fault, just like my old stories aren't my fault."

Turning to the sky, I spoke out loud. "I don't know how this works, but, Eve, if you can hear me, I understand."

Seconds later, I felt someone at my side. Out of the corner of my eye, I saw a slight movement in the air. Looking around, I only saw nature, but my eyes could tell where the spirit being stood. It was much taller than me, but I felt safe and calm. Is it an angel?

I felt a message. Eve—no, it was many—they knew.

I arrived home and strolled through my garden, but my thoughts were on the message and the angel. The biofields of living people need restoration; spirit beings are surrounded by electromagnetic frequencies from cell phone towers or other sources as much as we are. Spirit beings would have biofields, wouldn't they? Wouldn't their energy need restoration too?

"God, I want to help restore the biofields of spirit beings in heaven who love you. Do I have their permission?"

I closed my eyes and listened with my heart; maybe the angel would answer me again.

An inner prompt said, "Open your eyes."

The garden looked the same; I felt the prompt again. "Look with spiritual eyes."

With a heart full of desire, I looked into the air around me without focusing on anything and tried to hear or feel for something. A tiny bit of light or movement caught my attention from the corner of my eye. I turned to see what it was; twinkling orbs of light surrounded me twenty feet away! The spirit beings radiated with love and spoke as one. "Yes!"

My heart pounded. How do I do a session for spirit beings? Had I misunderstood? Had I just imagined the angel, the messages, and the orbs of light? If I hurt them and God rejected me, I'd be blamed by the living and the dead! But I wanted to help.

I couldn't see them and didn't know how many beings there were, so I held the intention to tune them by using a hologram. Because I was scared to be in contact with beings who may not have my highest good in mind, I said, "This hologram only holds the energy or spirits of angels and ancestors who love the creator."

I dubbed them the Restoration Group and tuned them like a living person. The outer edge of their biofields had a more intense dissonance feeling than the people I'd tuned in person; it felt like touching the electric fence that had kept our cattle in the wheat field during the winter when I was growing up, but not quite as strong.

Somehow I knew they had lower voltage than they were meant to have. A frayed piece of the outer edge flapped outside the biofield as if it were slowly being dissolved. I heard the group's concern through the forks. "We might not survive!"

When the forks sounded dissonant or my body felt tension, I stayed in that place until the clear sound could be heard again or until my body felt a relaxing of tension, then I moved to the next pocket of stuck energy. At the end of the session, I was surrounded by light as the spirits in the Restoration Group hugged me with joy.

For their next session, I followed every inch of the outer

edge of the field with the fork. They had a toroid field just like ours—a donut shape! Dissonance was all around the outer edge; I felt it in my body like an intense static or the buzzing of a mild electrical shock.

An hour later, my arms were tired and my shoulders were tense. I said, "I don't think I'm helping you very much."

I felt their reply. "Everything you do helps."

During the next tuning, I found a dense pocket of energy near the throat on the right side of their hologram, the side containing their father's information. I felt energy release in the forks at the same time a strong release occurred in my own throat. My dad was part of the Restoration Group! Stuck energy released in him and in me at the same time!

I approached each Restoration Group tuning as a meditation, since I was working in their spirits, and asked God for guidance. I felt angels and ancestors surrounding me with joy and love. In the third session, I could feel individuals within the group, but they still spoke as one. Clearing energy inch by inch around the outer edge of their field took a lot of effort. I needed tools that could hasten their restoration and make it easier for me.

In their next session, I added my biofield and my husband's to the hologram, including our ancestral fields, and grabbed my new forks. Energy flowed in spirals; these forks made the frequency of the sacred spiral.

After tuning the central channel energy that flowed up and down in the center of their biofields, I sent the frequency around the outer edge of the hologram for several minutes.

When dissonance was gone, they were full of energy, and I was too!

I continued to receive sessions from myself and other practitioners; as stuck emotions were released, my energy level increased, and I could more easily focus on the present moment as I tuned others. When working in people's biofields, I felt surrounded by spirit; I often felt the presence of an angel, and my intuition gave me information as I cleared energy. Working in spirit and meditating daily deepened my connection with God; the void I'd always felt inside was being filled.

Grandpa had been dead for almost twenty-five years when he stood beside me in my kitchen one morning. He looked directly at me. "I want to join the Oneness. I need your help."

My ears didn't hear his voice, but I understood what he said. I only saw him in my mind, but my eyes followed his energy. He was in grayscale—without color. I assumed he had a biofield, but I couldn't feel light around him like I could around individuals in the Restoration Group; they glowed with energy and life force.

Grandpa was wearing his usual farmer overalls but looked fifty years old, not the ninety-two he was when he died. He acted just like he did when he was alive; I felt his humor, sincerity, wisdom, and love for me. But he didn't have the joy and love for the universe like the Restoration Group did.

Working with the Restoration Group had shown me that the spirits of people who loved God still existed after they died. Grandpa had never attended church or talked about spiritual ideas. Am I safe talking to dead people? Why is this happening to me? And what is the Oneness?

Growing up in the Christian faith, I had heard about a fire-and-brimstone hell and a loving God; I had believed in both. But when I was in my early forties, my women's Bible study group had studied the Prayer of Jabez; I had said it in my own words every day. "God, please bless me and increase my boundaries. Be with me and keep me from evil. Grant me the desires of my heart."

Within weeks, I had ended a relationship that didn't meet my needs anymore. Within a few years, I had changed churches, changed careers, learned deeper spiritual truths, and married my husband, who desired truth as much as I did.

Convinced that most teachings maligned the character of a creator who was only truth, love, and free will, we had left religion and rewritten many of our beliefs. My daily prayer had become a deep yearning. "I want to know everything You want me to know; I want to know You!"

And now, Grandpa was in my kitchen, waiting for an answer. Did all my beliefs about death and the afterlife need to be rewritten?

I said to the universe, "Should I tune Grandpa's biofield, or clear his stuck energy within mine?"

# Chapter 4

# My Ancestors

The pendulum I used was just an acrylic ball; it spun from a string in my hand as spirit informed my mind. Grandpa was my mother's father, so I struck the forks on the left side of my hologram, where my mother's ancestral information was stored, and cleared all the stuck energy that presented. When I reached a stream of ancestral DNA, the grief Grandpa had felt when his oldest son died poured through me.

When the session was over, I didn't know what to do next, so I left the room.

Grandpa followed me. His vibration was calm and satisfied; he looked me in the eye. "Thank you."

Still scared to speak, I glanced toward him. What am I doing working with dead people? What happens now? He left my house.

The next morning, something inside me knew he was with

the other ancestors of the Restoration Group. But I felt guilty for being too wrapped in fear to enjoy seeing him again, and I missed him. I spoke aloud, hoping he would hear. "You're welcome."

In the coming weeks, intuition often directed me to clear stuck energy outside my biofield or those of my clients. Contacting other energy workers, I learned everyone had an ancestral biofield that extended up to thirty-five feet away from their body and contained the life record of all their ancestors. A person's father's ancestral information was on the right side of the ancestral field, and the mother's was on the left. My ancestors are part of me! I need to restore them to restore me.

My mother was still living, but I tuned my ancestral field to clear some of the stuck energy we shared. All her ancestors were deceased; a scrapbook showed their pictures, names, and a few details of their lives through the fourth generation.

My father was already in the Restoration Group, but I cleared my ancestral field for his patterns of unworthiness, regret, and not feeling good enough; his voltage seemed higher, and his vibration felt happier afterward, and I did too. My mother and an older cousin provided information about his ancestors.

Assuming the Oneness was where individuals of the Restoration Group existed—perhaps heaven—and that others who had died would need my help like Grandpa had, I invited my ancestors who were ready to go to the Oneness to be present while I cleared their energy. I completed a biofield session for one grandparent at a time, so I would be able to know which old beliefs and patterns came from which ancestor.

Like Grandpa, they came in grayscale with low voltage, with the personality they had when they were living. They expressed the same emotions and thought patterns I struggled with. I didn't physically see them in front of me, but my eyes tracked their energy. They came from a place where they had been waiting, and they wanted to go to the Oneness. After their sessions, I felt their higher voltage; none of them came back to try again.

My paternal grandfather died before I was born, but Dad had spoken of a drinking problem that often kept his father away from his family. Grandfather said with sadness, "I wasted my life."

I said, "Your life wasn't wasted; you gave my dad to the world! He was loved by many people, and he loved his family. Because of him, I am here today helping restore you and your family."

Regret for things I wished I had done or said differently had run nonstop during my life; after I cleared Dad's and Grandfather's energy, the hamster wheel slowed.

As I tuned my maternal grandmother, I found that red hair wasn't all I had inherited from her; she was my source of deep sadness too. She stood beside my hologram as I cleared the grief she had felt at eleven years old when her mother died, and at forty-seven when she lost her oldest son.

We raised her voltage enough for her to enter the Oneness,

and raised my voltage too. We held each other. "Grandma, I love you so much."

I cleared the loss my paternal grandmother had felt as her father died when she was a teen, the bottled-up anger and shame she felt as a young woman when she was taken without her consent, the unworthiness she had instilled in herself and her children, and the sorrow of losing some.

Then I tuned her father, clearing the emotions that had become stuck as he died. He said to me, "I loved my family so much."

One great-great-grandfather didn't come to his session, but in his energy in my ancestral field, I found the fear of rejection that had plagued my life. I felt the kicks and punches of his opponent landing on me as the two young men angrily rolled around in the dirt.

Later, as I cleared energy from his elderly years in my ancestral field, his stuck energy vibrated of unworthiness and anxiety as he lay on the floor of his house. His energy slowed to a stop as he died. In a second, I was looking through his eyes as he walked to the front door and opened it. Sunlight filtered in. Other grayscale ancestors stood in the shadows of trees at the edge of the yard and watched in silence. He closed the door and faded into the darkness.

An aunt appeared as I tuned my ancestral field; she had taken care of her younger siblings but had never had children or a home of her own. As I worked in a pocket of energy from when she was sad and dying in a care home, she said, "I took care of everyone else, but when I was in need, no one took care of me."

My heart jerked; I couldn't see to strike the fork. "I'm with you now; I'm taking care of you now."

A few minutes later, in my own field, I was crying again as I cleared energy that had become stuck when I had been taking care of my own children during a difficult time in their lives, but I had wanted someone to take care of me.

My ancestral field held the record of the death of an uncle who didn't have children; he came to transition. "Sometimes I was like a father to your dad when our father was not around."

In every session, I grew in compassion and understanding for each ancestor; I enjoyed the interconnectedness of our lives. Love flowed like a river through all generations—past, present, and future.

As I thanked them for their lives and sent them on their way to the Oneness, some of them wanted to stay. They seemed confused, like they expected me to do something else, but I insisted they leave. Where was the Oneness? How do they get there?

# Chapter 5

# The Universe

Focusing on the present moment, I held the intention of finding out more about the Oneness and asked for divine guidance. I tuned my own biofield and sent the fork's frequency around the outer edge of my hologram. When the energy was clear, I added my ancestral field to the hologram. When the energy at the edge of both biofields was flowing with ease, I said to the universe, "Is there a third biofield?"

Listening carefully with all my senses, I heard increased dissonance in the forks and felt different vibrations in my body. It was nature! It held the biofields of the earth, the sky, people, and all other living creatures. I felt stars too. Ancestors who died stayed in nature also; it was their waiting place.

In my mind, I set aside my own biofields and reduced the hologram of nature to the size of a human biofield, struck the tuning forks, found the outer edge of the biofield, and followed the electrical charge of nature around to where I started. Nature had a toroidal field too.

As I continued to work only in the biofield of nature, the pendulum indicated energy blocks near the top of the biofield. The dissonance felt like electromagnetic damage in the stratosphere above the earth, so I cleared the stuck energy in every direction around the central channel.

Adding my biofield and ancestral field back into the hologram with the biofield of nature, I held the forks at the outer edge of the field until the energy flow was smooth and clear. Then I said to the universe, "Is there a fourth biofield?"

Again I felt increased energy, as another biofield was added to the hologram. This one glowed with love and joy just like the Restoration Group! I could feel the individual biofields of ancestors who had transitioned; angels who vibrated with wisdom and love were there too. The Oneness was a biofield!

Within the top of the biofield of Oneness was a smaller field that overlapped into the biofield of nature; it held the sun and moon. Within the bottom of the Oneness was another smaller field that overlapped nature also; it held a large pool of concentrated energy.

I placed my forks at the outer edge of the hologram until dissonance was gone, then said to the universe, "Is there a fifth biofield?"

I waited, sensing beyond the Oneness. Instead of the increased dissonance of another biofield, I expanded into unending living energy—the field of light particles from which everything was made!

Every biofield in the universe was separate but couldn't exist separately. They were within each other—integrated, overlapping, of different sizes and capacities, and with distinct outer edges—but each only functioned as part of the whole.

The vibration of the universe held something else too, but I couldn't determine what it was.

# Chapter 6

# Ley Lines

Early in the morning, I ran barefoot in the garden; the rush of starlight that had soaked into the earth flowed through me and into the sky. I turned around slowly, looking at each tree and bush with the intention of lighting it up and renewing its energy; joy surged through me too.

One day, I overheard part of a podcast. "The earth retains the emotions of people who live on it; trees will tell you what the land feels."

I went outdoors, placed my hands on a tree, and quieted my mind; energy flowed over me, straight up and down. In a few seconds, I was smiling. The tree felt happy.

Days later, I stood next to another tree in our garden; I placed one of my arms around its trunk and both hands on its bark. My mind was clear of any thought except to feel anything I could; I breathed deeply. Suddenly, I was giggling. This tree was happy too! I tuned it with my forks, but I didn't feel the energy and interaction as strongly as when I just held the tree and listened.

Walking through our yard touching each tree, I said, "Thank you for being a beautiful part of our yard," or, "Thanks for your shade, for being shelter for the birds and animals."

Holding a strand of flowers on a shrub, I said, "I'd like to feel your energy."

A soft wave of energy flowed through me, as gentle and lovely as the flowers. I said, "You're beautiful! Thank you."

Still holding the strand, I turned to go, but the vibration was trying to tell me something!

It said, "I'm glad you care."

Tears filled my eyes. "Thank you for wanting me to."

On summer solstice, a picture on Facebook showed energy workers tuning ley lines. The only things I knew about ley lines were that they were naturally occurring streams of energy that could be found around the world, often near rivers, and that some people thought ley lines had magical or spiritual power. We live on the edge of an old river valley; I bet there's one within twenty miles that I could try tuning!

Walking into the garden a few feet from my house, I held the intention of tuning a hologram of the nearest ley line. I struck the fork and let it vibrate in front of me. Wooosh! Energy flowed through the hologram inches in front of me.

Two days later, an idea popped into my mind; I sent an

email to the host of a podcast I followed. "Would you be interested in having free biofield sessions?"

He responded quickly. "Yes, maybe next month."

Two more days went by; their latest prerecorded podcast was about tuning forks and sound vibration; they had interviewed the person on solstice!

Another of their podcasts later that week mentioned ancestors; I contacted them again. "There's a connection between biofield work and ancestors . . ."

The following week, an energy worker who had heard my interview on the podcast called to schedule a session, then changed the topic. "Your voice is only a partial tone; you need to ground your throat chakra to a ley line."

In every session, I connected the energy centers of the central channel to the earth and sky, but I had never heard of tuning one to a ley line. "I don't know much about ley lines, but I tuned a hologram of one when I was in my garden and heard a whooshing sound. Do you think it may be close?"

She paused. "I can feel a ley line on your property."

I stood where I had felt the wooshing; my skin tingled. I walked slowly toward the house, feeling a tingle with every step. The energy seemed to enter the house. If it kept flowing in the same direction, Grandma's rocker, where I sat for meditation every morning, would be in its path. Is that why I've had visions and traveled to the past and the future in my mind during meditation?

Sitting on the wooden floor with eyes closed and attention

on my throat chakra, I grounded my voice to the ley line. Energy danced through me, and I moved with it, grounding all seven energy centers. The next day, my voice sounded a bit less raspy.

The next week, I received an email offering a free course on basic energy dowsing. I had only heard of using dowsing rods to find underground water, not energy. The introductory video mentioned ley lines, so I signed up for the online class and learned about several different kinds of energy lines that flowed across the earth. In one video, ancestors transitioned at a positive vortex—a place of very high positive energy where two ley lines intersect at a ninety-degree angle.

Grabbing my pendulum, I ran outside to where I felt the wooshing energy again and asked the universe to help me find a ley line. The pendulum swung to mark both edges of the stream of energy; the ley line was five feet wide where it flowed into the house. As I walked around the house slowly, the pendulum swung again; the second ley line was eighteen inches wide where it entered the house!

Running back indoors with the pendulum, I marked the flow of both ley lines with tape; they intersected at a ninety-degree angle in the room where I worked! That's why some ancestors had looked confused and wanted to stay when I made them leave; they could have transitioned at that moment! I placed a large quartz rock in the center of the vortex to increase its voltage even higher.

One evening, I embraced the tree by our front door and held an intention to ground myself to the smaller of the two ley lines; it flowed a few feet behind me. The energy was strong, calm, and knowing.

I drew a quick breath; deep in the ley line was the concentrated presence of God! I said, "You're here!"

"Are you surprised?"

Having old beliefs ingrained in me, I still thought of God as being in the air, not the earth. "I didn't expect it! But I'm happy to know you're in the ley line."

"It is all good."

Did He mean all of creation or all His energy?

"It's all good with your life too."

I grounded myself to His presence in the ley lines every day, sitting in the vortex.

One day in meditation, He took me in a vision under the earth to where ley lines originated. A thick purple energy flowed like water and vibrated with the purest presence of God I'd ever known before; it was the energy from the smaller biofield at the bottom of the Oneness. I breathed this energy into my central channel, through my biofield, and into my ancestral field.

I said, "I've focused on breathing in earth's energy; is your energy better?"

"My energy from deep under the earth is more powerful, but all my energy is good."

I heard my ancestors in the Oneness. "We draw our energy from there!"

The deep energy had the same vibration I had always loved with all my heart, but this energy was not just around me—it was me! This was the energy I couldn't describe when I tuned the universe. The space between all the particles of light that all the energy in the universe was made of was not just air; it was spirit!

Just like me—where many charged particles of light combined into cells that made up tissues, organs, and systems of not just a fully functioning body but a sentient being—in all the light particles of everything everywhere in the universe was the spirit, intelligence, and personality that interacted with me personally and made me a sentient being!

The universe as a whole was the God I'd always yearned to be connected with—a conscious spirit with an unending expanse of energy, and a mind of abundance, safety, and free will! Gratitude overwhelmed me. I could never be rejected or alone; I was always worthy and always enough, because I was made of the Universal Spirit!

This knowledge was my power. Working in spirit every day, focusing on each present moment as often as I remembered, to keep both hemispheres of my mind working together in harmony, I felt safer, calmer, more confident, and more intuitive.

But many old thought patterns still distracted me and drained my voltage. As I continued tuning the Restoration Group, I added the biofields of nature and Oneness to the hologram; they seemed underpowered too. But ancestors in the waiting place had the lowest voltage.

# Chapter 7

# Ancestral Clearing

During sessions of self-tuning and tuning clients, ancestors came from both sides of families. Those on the mother's side stood to the left of my massage table; the father's ancestors stayed on the right. Sometimes only one or two appeared, but occasionally hundreds transitioned. Ancestors usually came alone, each one having made their own choice. They were ready to leave the waiting place—the biofield of nature—and go to the Oneness.

Sometimes a husband and wife or a parent and child stood near each other—like my great-great-grandmother, who came with her two-year-old son who had died of typhoid fever two weeks before she did—as if they had agreed to come at the same time or had the same patterns of stuck energy needing to be cleared.

My eyes tracked their energy; some were tall, some short.

The vibration of men differed from women. They entered at doorways and moved as if walking quickly, but they didn't touch the floor. A cool breeze came with them, making me shiver.

Though I usually only sensed their presence and felt their energy, my mind saw them. Ancestors from the waiting place were grayscale, like a flashlight with a battery running out of charge. Unlike ancestors in the Oneness, who radiated with the light, joy, and love of unlimited Universal Spirit, sometimes I saw grayscale ancestors dressed in clothing from the era in which they lived. Like fig leaves covering Adam and Eve, they were clothed with the mindset of lack and hierarchy they felt while living.

After I discovered that there was a vortex in my living room, I said aloud to all my ancestors whom I had known or heard about, "If any of you in the waiting place want to join the Oneness and don't have descendents, I'll help you go there when you're ready."

One cousin came with questions. "Did you know my parents?"

"Yes, I knew them well."

"Why do you do this work?"

"I want to help restore the universe, and I want people to know their oneness with Universal Spirit."

His glowing smile and the peace and love of the Oneness surrounded me as he left.

A girl who died very young was anxious and wanted a hug. "I might be all alone there."

"The Oneness is a wonderful place; your grandfather is already there."

She smiled and ran to the vortex.

One ancestor appeared in my garden but stayed fifty feet away. I felt his hesitancy; he wasn't sure he'd be welcomed. It was an uncle! I said, "It's so good to see you again!"

His vibration changed to joy and love as we entered my home.

One day, I recognized an ancestor instantly even though he had died before I was born. "I'm so glad to meet you!"

I continued talking about stories I'd heard of him, but sensed "blah, blah, blah" from his vibration; he was tired of the delay and wanted to be in the Oneness.

Over the course of several days, the attention—not the presence—of my ancestors from distant generations formed lines on both sides of my head. One day the pressure was between my eyebrows and couldn't be ignored; it extended in a long row behind me, as if they were waiting to be set free. My words flowed without conscious thought. "Every ancestor of mine since life began who is ready to join the Oneness, come now."

Energy poured out of my third eye chakra; many ancestors stood in front of me. The pressure behind my eyebrows was gone; both sides of my head felt spacious and open. I said,

"Thank you for all you've done and for being part of my life. You are released."

My body wiggled and squirmed as they transitioned; seconds later, a joyful thank-you came from the Oneness.

Ancestors from closer generations emitted a stronger vibration of love or tension than ancestors of long ago; parents usually had the strongest vibration. Often I asked more questions. "Are you a parent? A grandparent? Are you on the grandmother's or grandfather's side? Are you from the third generation or the fourth? Or further back?"

If intuition didn't tell me who they were, and my client knew some of their ancestor's names, I said to the ancestor, "Are you (name)?"

My mind, not my ears, heard the vibrations of their thoughts and feelings, and interpreted them into English in complete sentences. If I didn't understand words in response to my questions, my head automatically shook a 'no' if that was their answer. If it was the person I named, whether by ancestral position or given name, I felt 'yes' as a higher voltage between us.

Curious ancestors moved toward my laptop to see their loved one on Zoom or check out technology they had never seen. Some asked questions. "What are you doing?" or "What is this process called?"

One ancestor was very private and suspicious, not allowing his energy to clear. I said to my friend in the hologram, "Send him love or gratitude for being here; it'll help build his trust."

In another session, my eyes narrowed, lips pressed together, and hands tensed on the forks in response to one grandfather. I said to my friend on the massage table, "Send him love; let him know you want him here."

Halfway through the session, his anger and rudeness crumbled as release poured into my hologram. He said, "Thank you so much for helping me."

Another ancestor came to a session angry and antagonistic, blocking energy from clearing. I said to him, "You came by your own free will; you can go back to the waiting place if you want to. You're not welcome here unless you're ready to transition."

His energy softened; soon he relaxed, his stuck energy cleared, and he transitioned.

One ancestor said to his descendent, "Do you really want me in your life?"

My friend expressed sincere love and appreciation, and the ancestor's energy brightened.

As I removed pain from a friend's knee, energy pulled the fork near her heart; I cleared emotional pain. She said, "It isn't all mine; it's my grandma's pain too."

Her grandmother's energy entered the room; as we worked in the ancestral field, all three of us were crying. As I held the fork in a pocket of dissonance, my friend said to me, "My grandmother's mother died in front of her when grandma was a child."

"But this energy became stuck when she was an adult."

The grandmother said, "I brought all the emotion from childhood with me to this age; I couldn't let go of it before then."

Guided by intuition, I said to my friend, "I need you to hum; any song is okay. Or just make 'ah' or 'ohm' sounds to help this clear."

Waiting in the vortex, her grandma said, "My mother used to hum to me."

Another friend had lower back pain, but she wanted to help her ancestors instead of clearing her own pain. Her paternal grandfather joined us and said to me, "Ask her if she has happy memories of me."

I relayed the message, and my friend told stories of happy childhood times.

I said to her, "He's so glad to know you appreciate him!"

Still clearing energy in the ancestral field, I said to the grandfather, "Why are we working in the sacral area?"

He said, "When I was young, I hurt my back doing something I wasn't supposed to be doing. I never told anyone."

My friend texted me the following week. "My back hasn't hurt at all since the session!"

At another session, a friend said, "My grandmother died a few months ago. Last night, I smelled her hair spray, and later I heard the toilet flush even though no one was in the bathroom."

The grandmother joined us; they shared a loving goodbye without needing me to interpret.

At the end of every session, I asked each friend to send their ancestors to the Oneness with a prayer or blessing of gratitude, love, or compassion for the ancestor's contribution to his or her life. In return, ancestors often expressed dreams or longings. Some said, "I love you so much; I'm proud of you," or, "I'll help you from the Oneness."

One ancestor placed his attention, not his presence, in the pocket of his stuck energy I was clearing and said to me, "I'm not ready to transition, but please tell my granddaughter thank you for helping me."

Like my grandpa, some ancestors who died at an old age seemed much younger. Toddlers were usually two or three feet tall, and they often stood as if hiding behind their mother's skirts. Baby ancestors sometimes appeared as a child a few years old, but usually were at floor level and moved slowly, as if they were crawling.

One baby didn't speak in words, but I sensed his vibration. "I want to experience human love."

I picked him up, and my friend joined in a hug through Zoom, giving love to her child. The baby's vibration turned to satisfaction, then love, and soon he transitioned.

In one session, I was stuck in a pocket of regret. My friend said, "I lost a baby; I like to think it was the daughter I always wanted."

A little girl's voice—not her presence—came from the waiting place. "I wish I was with you."

One friend wanted emotional healing from miscarriages; as

I tuned her heart chakra, five babies entered the room. "How many times have you been pregnant?"

"Five. Years ago, a man told me he had seen babies in my aura and released them to God, but I've always regretted that I couldn't give them my love and say goodbye."

The babies were not vibrating with joy and love, but I asked them just to be sure. "Do you need to transition, or are you already in the Oneness?"

As the babies lined up at the vortex, my friend, hundreds of miles away, gave her children all her love for them. In response, their love flowed past me and directly into the phone. "Thank you, Mommy."

One day, a tall teenage ancestor appeared at my side. "I'm ready to transition."

I didn't know who he was until he began skipping beside me, lifting his knees high, taking long steps; his father had skipped the same way as a teen.

A grandfather came to be cleared. I coughed nonstop; the air seemed full of smoke. My friend said, "He died of lung cancer."

Sometimes, as I worked, I had visions, and my mind saw the ancestors in color, not grayscale. I saw and felt what was happening to them as if I was them at that moment in their lives. Several times I was an ancestor dying in bed as families gathered in front of me. I was a friend's uncle when he burned to death at ten years old.

Stuck in a pocket of energy during one session, I yelled, "Fire! I'm surrounded by fire!"

My friend said, "My great-great-grandmother died when her dress caught on fire."

In one vision, a friend's grandfather was a young boy with long dark hair, wearing blue overalls but no shirt; I ran through tall grass, fell, and cried as I hit the earth. As the session ended, his spirit flowed upward to join the bright orbs in the Oneness.

I was learning a lot about working with ancestors, but I knew it was just one aspect of all that was possible to experience through the light waves of the universe. I wanted to be able to receive all the intuition and guidance from Universal Spirit and all the resources the universe sent me. I wanted to see and hear and feel everything my spirit was aware of.

# Chapter 8

# Activating My Senses

Every morning I imagined feeling energy flowing from above my head and downward into my heart chakra with every breath I took, and from the heart to below my feet with every exhale. Reversing the pattern, I held the intention of sending the energy back through my central channel and out the top of my head.

As I focused on breathing through my central channel one morning, a tingling at the back of my neck and shoulders made me wiggle. The next day, I felt the wiggle at my mid-back, then at my lower back. Inhaling again, energy flowed from my crown to my tailbone, and then to my feet. With the next cycle of breath, I felt energy flowing through my central channel!

Many days, when breathing through my central channel, I noticed weakness, discomfort, or choppiness in my breath, as if it hit bubbles or pockets of stuck energy. Placing my attention on each energy center where I felt a block, I inhaled and exhaled through the central channel until each pocket dissolved and energy flowed smoothly through the chakras between the top of my head and my feet.

Throughout my house, I rearranged furniture, chose new paint colors, and placed décor items using basic feng shui ideas to increase my senses and intuition as well as the positive energy flow in each room.

I eased into yoga slowly using a chair to sit on or balance me, and breathed up and down my central channel until my breath moved smoothly through my body in every exercise. Slowly I gained flexibility and balance, became calmer, and could think more clearly.

Expanding my breathing exercises to include my spiritual chakras, I inhaled from the chakra three to four feet above my head, into the chakra fifteen to twenty inches above my crown, then through the top of my biofield, into my crown, and down to my heart. I exhaled from my heart down through my feet, then through the bottom of my biofield, and further down to the spiritual chakra fifteen to twenty inches below my feet.

Each day, to remind myself I was spirit, I focused on having an awareness of my biofield, five to six feet around my body, and placed my attention on the spiritual chakras inside and outside the outer edge of my biofield. As I walked through a dimly-lit room before sunrise one morning, little bits of light sparkled around me!

During meditation, Universal Spirit said, "Walk with me; learn my ways and heal my people."

"Where do I learn it? How do I do it?"

"It's inside you."

Fascinated with the idea of using my emotions to connect with spirit in the universe around me, I practiced by thinking of someone I loved until I felt love, then thinking of something that brought me joy and added joy to my vibration of love. One by one, I added the feelings of wonder, awe, intense gratitude, and curiosity of what connecting with the universe would be like.

Feeling all these high vibrations, I turned my attention to the sky. Looking past the physical world and into the spiritual, I said to the universe, "I want to see what you're really like; please show me."

Every day became an adventure, as I glimpsed sparkles or felt swirls and spirit presence around me. Experimenting barefoot in my garden by sensing vibrations after a thunderstorm and hugging trees for more energy, I said to a tree, "Do you have a word for me?"

The wisdom of the universe was in the tree. "We long for you just as you long for us."

As I sat in Grandma's rocker in the vortex one morning, Universal Spirit took me in a vision to a beautiful garden; the whole earth was before me. Giant trees acted as living Tesla towers, conducting the vibration of crystals in the earth through their leaves to recharge the energy of the universe. The leaves were as long as my hand, thick and narrow, with pointed ends; they stayed green and vibrant long after being picked. People placed leaves in their homes to feel the energy; some traveled far distances to obtain them.

The trees maintained the high voltage of the angels and ancestors in the Oneness, and recharged the energy of the people on earth who wanted it. These trees represented people's spiritual connection with the angels in the Oneness.

Later, I said to a friend, "I want to increase my senses to feel a deeper connection with spirit."

She said, "Years ago, I toured pyramids and artifacts of Egypt. Anthropologists in the group agreed the ancient hieroglyphics indicated that humans had three-hundred-sixty senses."

A picture flashed in my mind, and tingles ran through my body. "The hieroglyphics are referring to the human biofield—it's a three-hundred-sixty-degree sensing system! That's what the giant trees were for; people received a daily biofield session if they chose to tune into the tree's vibrations with their spirit. But people forgot they were spirit beings, and the trees were cut down."

Later that day, I activated a spiral vibration with my forks to amplify the sensing system of the universe for the highest good of all. The most powerful group of beings possible—the Oneness—held the intention with me. Following intuition, I tuned the biofields of all the parts of the universe to the whole of Universal Spirit, adding crystals to represent frequencies the giant trees would have provided. A pattern of energy flowed vertically and horizontally throughout the hologram, spiraling inward from the universe and outward from each part. As the session ended, my biofield was buzzing; ancestors in the Oneness were glowing!

As I stepped into the vortex, my laughter filling the room, Universal Spirit said, "Good job! I love you."

But I knew that to receive all that the universe was sending me, I had to clear more of the stuck energy that was causing roadblocks in my energy flow. I needed to clear the old stories my formative mind had believed as truth, and I wanted to know what experiences had caused the stuck energy.

# Chapter 9

# Trauma

Sadness flooded over me as I received a biofield session; the practitioner was stuck in a pocket of energy from when I had felt fat and out of control at age ten. In a vision, I saw my younger self, curled in a fetal position in the dark; she was crying too.

I said to her, "I'm so sorry I rejected you; I want you with me forever."

She uncurled and climbed out of the darkness and into my heart; we became one.

A few days later, fear overwhelmed me. I placed my attention into it, and suddenly was in a vision. I felt the fear of being unwanted and unworthy that I had felt in the womb.

Then, I felt my old thought pattern wanting to be in charge. "You're bad; I need to fix you."

Fear rose again. Taking a deep breath, I held the baby with my heart. "I love you so much. Please trust me. Give me your fear."

Smiling, she climbed into my lap, then into my central energy channel.

I said, "Thank you for trusting me; thank you for letting me love you now."

In another session a few weeks later, the practitioner said, "In this stuck energy, you're three years old and feeling terror."

"I don't remember anything that would have caused terror at that age; I don't feel any emotions right now."

"In my experience, people who have blocked out memories of sexual trauma from when they were young usually have body image problems by the age of ten and have eating disorders in their teenage years."

The first thought that came to mind was a memory I was ashamed of. "When I was a child, I often played with my Barbie doll behind a large chair in the corner of the dining room where no one could see me; I'd take off her clothes and place her on a little table. The two boy dolls would laugh at her and rub their hands between her legs. I never knew how I learned to play that way, but I always felt guilty for it."

That night, I said to Universal Spirit, "Please give me a memory."

Two days later, I was in a vision. I was little, wearing a dress and lying on a table. A man stood at my right side wearing dark pants and a white shirt; his face looked familiar. Somehow, I knew his wife was aware of what he was doing, but she wasn't there. A half-grown boy stood at my left knee.

Weeks later, as a practitioner worked in my biofield, anger ripped through me. When her fork sounded dissonant in the ancestral flow on my right side, I said, "I hear the man from my three-year-old terror; he's sad the little girl was scared, but he doesn't regret what he did."

My father and all my grandfathers in the first four generations had already transitioned. I didn't have a father-figure other than my dad; this man must have been a father figure to Dad.

The practitioner said, "For this session, we held the intention to help your relationship with money; maybe the man gave you money."

I was still angry, but, knowing that if my life had been different, I may not be connecting deeply with Universal Spirit and having the experiences I am now, I said to the man, "Thank you for what you did."

"Do you mean it?"

Part of me did.

The next week, I said to a friend, "I haven't done hypnosis before; I'm nervous."

"Nothing can happen that you don't want to happen. Let's do a practice session so you can feel more comfortable with the process."

He walked me down a stairway and into the sunshine, then to a tree near a stream. The tree said, "Sit."

The grass said, "Take off your shoes and feel the ground."

My spirit was part of the ground, then I was the tree. It was the cottonwood that had been cut down when I was young; seeing the tree lying in the dirt that day had broken my heart. I had played in its shade: hopscotch, hide-and-seek, tag. My young arms had not been able to reach around it, but I had placed my hands on its trunk and talked to it; it had been my friend.

Being near the tree again made me feel safe and comforted. "Tree, do you have a name?"

"No. I *am*."

As my friend guided me, I looked for angels, ancestors, or animals, but only saw the tree, the light, and me. "Tree, will you go with me on my journey?"

"No, the light is all you need."

"Light, will you show me your heart?"

"You are my heart."

I climbed into a small travel pod; it landed on a beautiful beach. The water held crystals, and dolphins that healed people. Floating through the water, surrounded by light, I spoke with the dolphins without words, touching them softly.

Soon I returned to the bottom of the stairway. The tree, light, and water had felt so safe; I wasn't ready for the uncertainty of the world.

"Tree, will you come with me?"

"No. You have all you need inside you."

In my next hypnosis session, I was three years old, standing in the dining room of the farmhouse I grew up in; the wood floors and dinner table were dusted with the light pouring in through tall windows.

I walked across the gray-tiled kitchen floor, out the back porch door, and down the wooden steps to my cottonwood tree. I rode in the back seat of a car for a long time.

My conscious mind recognized the man who walked up to the car; my family had visited him several times when I was growing up. As my parents went into the house with his wife, the man turned to me, speaking softly. "You're so pretty. Come with me."

My bare feet walked through the grass to a building; he opened the door. He placed me on a table and stood at my right side; I felt his hands under my dress, the tip of his finger inserted between my legs.

He looked toward the door. "Boy! Come here!"

A half-grown boy entered the room and stood at my left side. He said to the man, "You shouldn't be doing that, it's wrong!"

The man looked at the floor. "I know."

He helped me off the table and gave me a coin. "Go buy some candy."

In the yard, my big brother came running; he was almost five. "I heard you crying and wanted to help, but the door was locked. Are you okay?"

We walked to the house. Mommy and Daddy were there with my baby sister and the man's wife. In my conscious mind, there flashed scenes of when I had tried to be good to please Dad. The smiles of love on my parents' faces told me they had no idea that anything had happened. But the woman was angry; she knew, but said nothing.

Hypnosis helped me understand the source of some of my old emotional reactions and thought patterns, but I needed acknowledgement of my pain. The man and his wife died thirty years ago. All I have are pockets in my biofield, memories of my Barbie doll, a vague vision, and hypnosis; I doubt my family would believe me.

I wrote a letter to the man's son and mentioned very few details, pretending that I didn't know what had happened and wanted his help to remember. As I slipped the envelope into the mail, I felt some of my ancestors in the Oneness. They said, "Thank you for writing the letter."

Weeks later, I awoke during the night. Still in bed, my head turned to the west; roads and terrain passed as I traveled. Knowing Universal Spirit was taking me to the son's house, I sent him love and support. The front room of his home was bright; pictures hung on the walls. He entered the room and wrote something on a piece of paper, wadded it up, and tossed it onto a pile in the wastebasket by his chair. Silently I said, "Write it all; let it all flow."

Intuition led me to a bookshelf; a manila envelope was in the middle of a tall stack of paper. Trying not to topple the stack, I tugged gently until the envelope was in my hands; it was nine by twelve inches. He won't want this; it's so much bigger than he needs.

His back was to me, but his thoughts said, "Yes, I'll use it."

I laid the envelope where he could find it and stood with my arm around his shoulders as he wrote, sending him thanks.

Processing my emotions of trauma took months, especially my feelings about money; I needed more information. In another hypnosis session, I was on the table; the man reached into his pocket, then extended his arm toward me. I could hardly see the coin pinched between his finger and thumb.

He said, "Never tell anyone or you'll be a bad girl."

The trauma had affected how I felt about my body, food, sex, relationships, and money. It brought distrust, unworthiness, fear of being rejected, and fear of speaking my truth. Anger, hate, sadness, and feeling unworthy had become anchored in my mind and in the muscles of my shoulders and back.

Emotions cleared a bit every day as I focused on where I felt them in my body. Yoga, massage, biofield sessions, crying, screaming, talking with my husband, and journaling helped.

As a three-year-old, my formative mind had said, "You're a victim. This vibration means you can't change what happens to you; you can't change how you feel about it."

Powerlessness was the lens through which I had viewed life. But having read that the vibration of fear was similar to the vibration of excitement, as I cleared emotions caused by trauma, I chose to feel my fear as excitement to help me step into my power, take action, and create the life I wanted.

In meditation, Universal Spirit took me inside my body

to the vaginal opening. Feeling the old trauma, I said to those muscles, "Release. Forgive."

Suddenly, in a vision, I was three years old. I said to the man as he touched me, "Stop it! You have no right to do this! Take your hands off me!"

Then I forgave him. And I forgave his son for not being able to stop him; I forgave my brother for not being able to help me. I said, "We're going into the house to tell Dad and Mom."

Still in the vision, I told my parents what had happened; my brother spoke also, and the son nodded in agreement. The man hung his head. I forgave my father for not protecting me, then I forgave my mother for not comforting me. As I released the feelings buried sixty years ago, gratitude for my family filled my heart.

Weeks later, in meditation with Universal Spirit, my feelings of love and joy drained away, and tingles spread across my body. The man was standing next to me. Anger boiled up. "Why did you hurt me! I hate you! I was just a little girl! You made me feel pain all my life!"

His vibration held sadness for the little girl who had been scared, but not sorrow for his actions.

But without his actions, I wouldn't be experiencing the wonders of the universe or feeling the wonderful changes within me that I am now. "Thank you for what you did."

"Really?"

"Yes."

He moved to the vortex. "I want to transition."

"You need to let your son know you want his help."

He said, "I'm ready for the Oneness."

No, he's avoiding his son. But maybe he can. "You're welcome to try."

He stayed in the vortex, wiggling, a vibration of frustration building.

I said, "Maybe you need to clear your heart."

He turned away into the waiting place.

# Chapter 10

# Wisdom

Knowing about my trauma and old stories helped me know where to focus on clearing stuck energy in my biofield. Though energy still jerked through me as I continued to clear my three-hundred-sixty-degree sensing system, after a few months of tunings, it flowed with much less static. Circuits were being restored! As I gained greater awareness of my biofield and remembered more often that I was spirit, I was able to feel the love and joy of nature and the Oneness surrounding me every day.

I practiced scanning the garden with my senses, then increased the distance to include the next block, then the edge of town; soon I sensed joy or confusion, safety or danger from miles away any time I stopped to listen. Intuition guided my work easily—words flowed in perfect timing, insights came often, synchronicities happened, and I seldom second-guessed my actions.

Driving through a city, I saw the spirit world, not just nature; tree energy danced with joy and excitement as snow blew through the air. Two weeks later, my own garden was a snowy world. Nature called me with wonder and happiness. "Come play with us!"

It was three degrees above zero, but I grabbed my coat. Energy flowed through me as I hugged a tree. It said, "Thank you for coming out. We love you so much."

My heart went to Universal Spirit. "Thank you for awakening me to your world."

On a spring night, the full moon filled my dining room with light. I was standing in the ley line, leaning against the window, but the energy was more intense than it usually was. I stepped outside to hug a tree; the energy running through my hands was alive and lighted my whole being. As I stood in the ley line, bathed in moonlight, my whole body was shaken to the core.

One day, I glanced out the car window; the stores and cars looked just like a toy set! Intuition flashed: fear and control are like toys; abundance and free will are reality! I blinked and looked again, but saw only the strip mall.

Feeling tired and emotional the next day, I found where I felt powerlessness again in my body. The old stories of feeling unworthy and thinking I had no choice in how my life played out were toys too.

After amplifying my sensing system in many sessions, I tuned my skeletal system to receive signals from the universe too, since energy flowed from the universe into the light waves of my biofield and throughout the connective tissue in my body. I used the forks to bring harmony to the parts of my brain, body, and chakras that specifically helped my senses. But energy of the parts of the brain existed within my biofield also; I wanted to tune them, but I didn't know where they were.

I said to Universal Spirit, "Please show me."

I named a body part, waited to be shown where it was in my hologram, tracked the energy with my eyes, and tuned each part to Universal Spirit. When I was done, energy buzzed through me.

But a deeper connection with the universe only pulled me to experience more, so I called another friend who did hypnosis. "I heard we come from the Oneness and return there between our lives on earth; I want to find out if it's true."

She guided me down a staircase and through a door. Surrounded by ancestors and angels, warm light, joy and love, I was not me. I was part of the light of the Oneness and fully loved, wanted, and needed.

Then I individuated, becoming my own spirit, but still surrounded by those in the Oneness. I had the awareness that I had not lived in a physical body before. Something drew my attention to the left; my parents' energies were swirling together. The Oneness said to me, "Do you want to join them?"

I knew that Universal Spirit wanted my help, so I moved toward them. Fourth of July sparklers lit around me! Lightly, a pressure touched me, placing limits on my biofield as my body formed. The joy, love, and gratitude of the Oneness were part of me, and I remembered being part of them.

Without warning, I was shaking with fear and sadness, and crying. "I feel so alone. I want to be back with the Oneness!"

The hypnotist asked, "What would help you feel better?"

"If Mommy wanted me."

As my friend guided me to breathe deeply, the fear and sadness eased, and calm returned.

The intense emotions I felt in the womb were difficult to experience, but I wanted more answers, so for our next hypnosis session, I gave my friend a list of questions.

She led me into being part of the Oneness again; I individualized and joined my parents. My expansiveness diminished as my body formed. Fear and sadness overwhelmed me again, then calm. She asked, "What do you feel now?"

"My parents are worried and rushing around."

I told her part of my birth story, "They were trying to get to the hospital during a snowstorm in the middle of the night."

Suddenly, I was being pushed out! My body wiggled on the massage table as I traveled the birth canal. I was surrounded by light; shadowy forms moved in front of me. Why are they laughing at me? I can't help how I look! Lying on my mommy, everything felt safe and good.

My friend read the next question on my list. "Do you see the placenta?"

In meditation, I had been shown that our body and placenta

together represented our whole sentient being—the physical and spiritual—and also our oneness with Universal Spirit. As I sensed into the hospital room, my subconscious mind took over. "Noooo! It's in the trash can! It's mine! I need it!"

My friend said, "Can you pick it up and hold it?"

Grabbing the placenta, I held it to my chest. "I hate them! I hate them!"

"Take a deep, slow breath. Hold it, hold it. Now slowly let it out."

My husband held me while my subconscious mind continued to scream. "I hate them! They knew what they were doing. They did it on purpose!"

My friend said, "Can you forgive them?"

"No! I can't!"

"I feel you're holding space for everyone who feels this separation of body and spirit. Can you let it go?"

Her question cleared my mind, and it heard my spirit. I listened to my body. "Yes."

But should I? Medical practice separates our wholeness at birth, just as the mindset of fear and lack keeps our minds from hearing our spirits most of our lives. I called into the Oneness for wisdom. "I'm holding space for everyone; do I have the right to let it go?"

An ancestor said, "You have acknowledged their pain; you can let it go."

I released the hate, fear, and hurt as I slowly exhaled until I was calm again.

Experiencing the Oneness was wonderful, and I wanted to ask more questions of the angels and ancestors there, but reliving the fear in gestation was too painful to visit again. I said to Universal Spirit, "Was my fear caused by coming into a physical body? Does everyone feel it? Or was it because I felt my mother's thoughts and emotions?"

Universal Spirit said, "Will you come with me?"

Entering my crown, Universal Spirit came with me into my third eye chakra. I was in the womb, just beginning to form; I was both an individual and still part of the Oneness, and in perfect harmony of mind and spirit. I felt my spirit's primary intention: to always know this Oneness with Universal Spirit.

But feeling fear for more than a few minutes, my protective mind had blocked my awareness of spirit, and I had felt alone; fear had been my mind's pattern of reaction all my life.

# Chapter 11

# Holding

Overwhelmed with worry for my grown children one day, I asked my ancestors in the Oneness for wisdom. Dad said, "I worried about your decisions, knowing you would hurt, knowing your children would hurt."

But I couldn't stop; it was making me ill. I said to Universal Spirit, "Help me! My mind won't stop!"

Universal Spirit's words were soft and kind. "Give it to me. Consciously choose to let me hold your mind."

My mind had forgotten I was spirit; I had forgotten that my emotions and memories were held at all times by Universal Spirit in the light waves around me.

Consciously choosing for my spirit to be in charge, I said, "Mind, you've worked so hard to keep me safe; thank you. But I don't want you to feel frazzled, so I'm giving you to Universal

Spirit, the one who holds all things. You're made of spirit; it's holding you. You're not alone; you're always safe, always held."

Immediately, my mind went deeply calm for several hours. Every time I felt the slightest hint of fight or flight worry begin, I lovingly said, "Mind, you are held by Universal Spirit."

Each time, worry stopped and gratitude filled my heart; I focused and thought clearly again, calm and free of fear.

After I tuned my biofield one day, several of my ancestors from generations long ago were ready to transition, but one drew my attention. Without thinking, words flowed from my mouth. "It's you! Thank you for all you've done!"

He must have had an important role in the world, perhaps like Abraham Lincoln! But why did I think of Lincoln? Did he look like Lincoln? He left in the vortex.

Weeks later, a friend announced she was expecting her first child. Knowing that in the womb, the baby's spirit would remember being in the Oneness, I said to Universal Spirit, "How can I help this baby remember that she's always part of the Oneness?"

"Hold her like I hold you."

Universal Spirit took me in a vision past the stars, sun, and moon. A little baby was very scared; it was me. I held her close. "Everything's okay, little one."

Universal Spirit said, "I held you when you were scared."

"When I was in the womb or during the trauma when I was three?"

"I hold you always, but in the womb, the mind soon forgets

being held. Parents used to hold the spirit's intention for their children beginning at conception, and teach them that they were part of the Oneness. Few people hold their future generations now."

Somehow knowing that Universal Spirit's "I" was "We," I said, "I'd like to meet the ancestor who held me."

As I stood in the Oneness, ancestors gathered in front of me; a path opened down the center. Again my words came without thinking. "It's you!"

The important work of my Abe Lincoln-type ancestor had been holding the intention for my spirit to remember that I was one with Universal Spirit!

I said, "Who are you?"

"My name doesn't matter; I'm from Tobias's clan."

During gestation, my mind had forgotten my Oneness, yet long before I was born, this paternal ancestor had held my spirit's intention for me. Was this why I had yearned for Universal Spirit all my life?

Universal Spirit took me within myself again to feel my spirit's intention being held for me. The vibration was loving and being loved at the same time; it was an affirmation of the Oneness my spirit already felt, a confirmation of my desire for the Oneness, and a reminder to keep my spirit in charge of my mind so that I could choose how to act instead of reacting from the fear of not having or being enough.

My friend's baby was just four weeks from conception. I focused my attention on feeling the joy of my ancestors in the

Oneness; while holding that feeling of joy, I connected with her spirit, my thoughts encouraging her to feel the Oneness. My spirit bridged any gap between her spirit and the love, joy, and gratitude of the Oneness. Feeling the sweetness of her pure vibration of love, I said her spirit's intention to her. "You are one with Universal Spirit."

I held her spirit's intention every day; at six weeks of gestation, a return vibration of love came from her! Soon I felt this connection every day; often, her attention flowed to my chair through the ley line and landed in my lap.

One day, at eight weeks into gestation, her vibration was sadness. As I sent joy, her sadness changed to joy.

Four months into gestation, something was different one morning. The return vibration was fight or flight—her energy was going around and around. She was scared. I connected with the Oneness and held her with their love and joy. I reassured her that she had all she needed, that she was always connected to Universal Spirit, and that her spirit was in charge of her mind. Her mind quieted.

One day, the baby's spirit said to me, "Why do you feel sad?"

"I'm not sad."

I was worried about money. Feeling lack led to my old story: I wasn't worthy of having enough money. But under the unworthiness in my body, I felt something else; baby was right—my spirit was sad that my mind didn't know I was enough.

Two weeks before the due date, the baby's attention was directed to her body as it prepared for birth. She felt uncertainty and fear. I sent her the vibrations of love and joy to help her connect with the Oneness. "Let the fear flow through you—let it go. Your birth is perfect timing."

Two days before her due date, her energy was completely focused on her mom. I said to Universal Spirit, "I know this is the way it should be, but I'll miss connecting with her spirit; my job is over."

"Your job is just beginning. Rest now and wait."

Baby and parents were at the hospital, but her attention was with me while I held her intentions that morning. She said, "It's dark and scary."

"Yes, it feels that way, but everything's okay; this is your birth. Focus on the Oneness."

I filled my heart with vibrations of love and joy to help her; she became calm.

Two days after she was born, her spirit heard my thoughts and remembered the Oneness as I held her spirit's intention, but she didn't recognize my individual vibration. Her mind didn't remember being held.

Without her personal connection, I held the spirit's intention for her and her family, for myself and my family, my relatives and friends, for everyone living and all future generations, and for all ancestors and angels in the waiting place and in the Oneness.

I held the intention for children, to help them remember

the feeling of being spirit so they would have fewer old stories and fewer patterns of fight, flight, or freeze. I held adults to help them live as spirit, feel a connection with the Oneness, be more at ease with life, and be able to transition into the Oneness at death. I held grayscale angels and ancestors to help them find their way to the Oneness much sooner. I held intentions for all those in the Oneness, including those who have not yet lived a physical life, to affirm the love I shared with them and to increase their voltage.

As I held the spirit's intention for the baby every day, and held the same intention for everyone in the universe, those in the Oneness held the intentions with me, amplifying the intention in all.

Intuition helped me see that the broad spirit's intention of knowing I was one with Universal Spirit had five parts; each part held an aspect of the energy represented in my five spiritual chakras.

The chakra fifteen to twenty inches below the feet represented the ascending flow from the concentrated energy of Universal Spirit deep under the earth. This chakra's intention was for each being to know that we are spirit beings. Our spirits' desires are to lead our minds.

The intention of aligning our minds to hear our spirit was in the spiritual chakra fifteen to twenty inches above the crown. It represented being able to recognize when our minds were at the point of choosing between hearing our spirits or reacting in a pattern of fight, flight, or freeze.

The chakra three to four feet above the crown represented

the descending current of energies from the Oneness: those who had the mindset of the abundance and free will of Universal Spirit and whose spirits always led their minds. The intention: we consciously choose to live as spirit.

The chakra just inside the outer edge of the biofield held the intention that we live in harmony with the abundance of the universe and know that everything the universe brings is good.

The chakra just outside the outer edge of the biofield represented knowing we came from the oneness and will return to the Oneness, and that only the full expression of each part fulfilled the whole. The intention: we are fully expressing ourselves for the highest good of all.

As I held the spirit intention for all, the universe poured into me. In response, my spirit broadcasted as a loud roar throughout the universe, holding space for all, because every spirit knew it was one with Universal Spirit. It was only their protective minds that had forgotten they were spirits.

Desiring all my loved ones to be happy, have fulfilling lives, loving relationships, and enough money for all their needs, I held their spirits' intentions because it was for their highest good. But I struggled with holding this broad intention for my children. Forgetting that every choice I had made in my life had worked for my highest good, I worried about them. I didn't want them to make mistakes like I did.

Forgetting to think about the joy and love they would feel when they aligned their mind with their spirits' intentions, I tried to vibrate with the happiness they would feel when they experienced the fulfilling life I wanted for them. I couldn't reach the vibration of joy, love, and gratitude needed for the intention to really be powerful.

I held a tree. "If what's happening in their lives is for their highest good, but my mind doesn't want it to happen, how can I vibrate with love, joy, and gratitude?"

Tree said, "Try carving."

"What?"

A picture came to my mind, hands carving a piece of wood into a figurine.

Tree said, "Carve."

"The larger piece of wood is the broad spirit's intention for our highest good? The figurine is the narrow intention that I hold the emotion for? By holding the broad intention I'm also holding the narrow one?"

Tree waited for me to understand.

Then I knew. "Whatever the universe brings from our spirits' intentions *is* our highest good! The emotion we need to hold to help the intentions manifest is the love, joy, and gratitude of knowing that the universe is always working for our highest good!"

Choices I saw as mistakes—mine and theirs—were meant to be; it was our free choice. Free choice meant to be because it's the mindset of Universal Spirit. Every choice we've ever made has moved us toward the Oneness and so has always worked for our good.

I knew that using my free choice to fully express my own

desires for the highest good of all would set my mind free to hear my spirit. Holding my children's spirits' intentions—not my own narrow desires for them—would help them express their individual desires and help set them free too!

# Chapter 12

# Generations

After holding their spirits' intentions for my descendents and ancestors one day, I realized how much I missed my younger son; he lived many hours away. I focused my attention and intention to connect with him.

His warmth, the scent of his cologne, and the usual inflections of his voice were suddenly real. "Hi, Mom."

His spirit was so close! I wanted a deep conversation to share the spiritual ideas I was learning, but only one thing mattered. "I love you."

I said it three times. A few minutes later he sent a text. "Hi Mom, how are you?"

I left a voicemail. Later I held a tree near our house while thinking of him; my spirit traveled west. I entered his front door, and my thoughts called his name; he was in the garage. My phone beeped with his text.

Weeks later, I felt overwhelmed all day. Several times, I listened carefully within me, but couldn't find tension from overwhelm in my body—it wasn't my emotion. That evening he called. "I had to see a doctor this week . . ."

One day, I awoke with an anxiety that felt like my mother's; I called her. "Mom, are you okay?"

She said, "I've been feeling really overwhelmed today; I have so much to do in the next few weeks, and I'm not as young as I used to be."

I imagined a pie chart sliced in half for my parents, in quarters for my grandparents, in eighths for my great-grand-parents, and so on, the number of ancestors in each generation growing larger as each individual ancestor's percentage within me grew smaller. Through DNA and spirit, the emotions, experiences, and wisdom of my ancestors were in me. I desired more connection with my ancestors in the Oneness, and they desired connection with me—a magnetism of all the parts for the whole.

Grandpa came from the Oneness one morning. "You asked Universal Spirit if the sun, moon, and stars work the way they were meant to work, and if they have the power they were meant to have. There's an ancestor I want you to meet; he knows things that you need to know."

The next day, I said to Universal Spirit, "How will I meet this ancient grandfather?"

Intuition answered; in hypnosis, I could see and feel as a participant.

During hypnosis, Grandpa met me in the Oneness. I said, "I would love to meet this ancestor and learn what he knows. Is he in the Oneness?"

"No, but his record is in you."

Within seconds, I was in a vision; the ancient grandfather was lying on the dirt floor of a dark cave. He looked frail, as if he had been starved. Then I was him; several men, dressed in the rough clothing of centuries earlier, entered the cave and struck me with wooden clubs. Scared and in pain, hands protecting my head, I screamed.

The hypnotist distracted me. "Is it you or your grandfather they're hitting?"

"Grandfather. But I feel it in my body."

"Can you watch what is happening without being a participant?"

I knelt at Grandfather's side as they beat him. His spirit said, "They're killing me because I know a secret, and they don't want others to know it."

His thoughts took me to an island. "This is the Welchland."

An old boat with mast and sails floated at a wooden pier in a cove surrounded by trees. We went through the hatch into the bottom of the boat; kneeling in front of a wooden chest with metal trim, I opened the lid and unrolled yellowed papers. I couldn't read the ancient writings, but I looked at sketches of circles and spirals that interconnected like pathways.

He said, "It shows how the moon works."

His presence was fading; back in the cave, I was him again, dying.

Still in hypnosis, when the vision ended, I said to the Oneness, "Can I learn more about how the sun, moon, and stars work?"

In a vision again, I saw the moon; it was in the biofield of Oneness, but its shiny energy moved like a pendulum within nature, from full to sliver and back again.

Days later in meditation, a vision took me back in time. I was my ancient grandfather, driving an open wagon on a dirt road between two cornfields; a man sat beside me. As we drove through a cave, men ran out of the darkness and stopped the wagon. The man sitting beside me grabbed me while the others pulled me from the wagon and threw me into the cave where they had killed him.

One morning, as I finished meditation, the ancient grandfather was waiting at my left side, ready to transition. I welcomed him with gratitude and watched him ascend.

Universal Spirit took me in a vision to see the sky clock—the sun, moon, and stars that set the times of nature. Within the biofield of Oneness, three or four suns were dark and full of sadness; each had a moon. In the distance, one sun and moon were shining.

The sky clock spread out evenly above the top of the biofield of nature, but the energy didn't feel right to me. Like my ancient grandfather's sketch, something seemed to fall across the moon, creating its phases. I said to Universal Spirit, "How does the moon work?"

In a biofield session a few days later, the sky clock was my hologram. The sun vibrated with pure power, but the energy of the stars was a network—an expansion of awareness. The central channel of its biofield was clogged with sadness; the sun, moon, and stars had not been able to recharge and feel the full power of the universe since the giant trees had been destroyed.

I found a shield over the heart chakra; the sky clock was sheltering itself from feeling greater loss. A ceiling was over the solar plexus, limiting its power. I worked until the shield and ceiling were gone and the biofield of Oneness that held the sky clock glowed with happiness.

Again Universal Spirit took me high above the biofield of nature, above the center of the earth; the sun and moon were far away, and everything else was dark. The sadness of the sky clock filled me; it wanted to be the light it was meant to be.

I said again, "How does the moon work?"

In a vision, I saw the drawings of my ancient grandfather. Like before, the vibration indicated that something was not right, and the moon was sad.

Led by intuition, I tuned the sky clock again, releasing stuck energy at the heart and throat chakras. I tuned all the parts of the universe to Universal Spirit, clearing huge pockets of sadness, grief, and the mindset of lack that had been felt when the entire universe reacted in fight or flight as the trees were cut down and the daily recharging of the universe ended.

As a continuous stream of ancestors from many generations transitioned after the session, I soaked up the joy, love, and gratitude of my ancient grandfather, all those in the Oneness, all of nature, and Universal Spirit.

I felt pressure and palpitations around my heart and third eye chakra all evening, but the next day I glowed with joy; I felt a great abundance of renewed energy fueling all of nature as it filtered through ley lines and dispersed in the universe.

My husband woke up humming, something he didn't do very often. He said, "You must have been tuning yesterday; I could feel energy clearing within me while I worked."

A friend said, "Yesterday, I was sad all afternoon."

I continued tuning myself and the universe every week for an abundance of energy and time; tunings during a solstice, full moon, and morning rain were best of all. In every session, I felt like I was being guided by an angel; after each session, I was hugged by all the celestial energies and beings in the Oneness.

# Chapter 13

# Gabriels

As the hypnosis session began, I said to my friend, "I would like to return to a time in my childhood when I was four years old."

"Tell me more."

"My mom told me that I came running up to her saying there was a man talking to me in the backyard. Mom was certain no one else was around the farm, so she had said to me, 'It's Jesus.' She'd been surprised by her response, because she didn't go to church then."

My friend said, "Was it Jesus?"

"From what I've learned of spiritual things, no, it wasn't Jesus. But I'd like to know who it was and what they said."

She took me back in time. "Tell me what you see."

"I'm at the picnic table in the backyard. A man covered with light is standing near me. He's very tall and strong."

"What did he say?"

"He said, 'You're wonderful; never let anyone tell you different.'"

"That's great! Did he say anything else?"

"Yes. He said, 'I'm your guardian angel. You'll know me as you seek wisdom when you're older. I'll be with you.'"

"What's his name?"

"Gabriel. But it felt like a title, not his name; I read somewhere that the word Gabriel means 'God is my strength.' He's a messenger for Universal Spirit. Angels are like trees; their energy reads, 'I *am*.' Gabriel knows who he is as part of the whole."

"Does he visit you now? Has he come to you again?"

"I don't see him, but he's in the Oneness, and sometimes I feel him helping me with the ancestors."

One day, as I held the vibrations of love, joy, and gratitude within me and looked with wonder and curiosity beyond what my eyes could see, a swirling motion ten feet away sparkled in the sunlight for a few seconds.

The next day, I held the vibrations again, wanting to talk to Gabriel. But instead of hearing words or feeling a presence, I only saw sparkling swirls again.

When I saw the swirls on the third day, I said, "Gabriel?"

"Yes."

Because the biofield of Oneness overlapped and encompassed that of nature, I was able to feel the angels of the Oneness in nature also. "Are you always with me?"

"Yes."

I smiled. "Thank you. I love you."

Before I went to sleep, I gently rubbed my third eye and crown chakras, holding the intention of learning more about angels. The next morning in meditation, Universal Spirit said, "You want to know more about the angels?"

"Yes."

Universal Spirit took me in a vision to the Oneness. I felt angels: a constant strong flow of energy similar to the 'I *am*' vibration of the trees but with a lower tone, a higher voltage, and much love. Then I asked to feel the vibration of ancestors in the Oneness. There was less movement—more of just being present—a higher tone, and more joy than love.

Often when giving biofield sessions, intuition was the energy of the universe coming as synchronistic thoughts or ideas at just the right time, showing me what to do or say, or physically moving me to where I needed to work. Sometimes I had a knowing, or my eyes automatically went to where the stuck energy needed to be released.

But sometimes my eyes tracked Gabriel's energy as he stood across the massage table from me. And when I heard words directing me what to do for the highest good of all, I knew it was Gabriel.

In one session, intuition directed me to work at the outer

edge of my friend's ancestral biofield; after several minutes, the energy hadn't cleared.

Gabriel said, "Try love."

I struck a fork often said to be the frequency of love and held love in my heart; the energy cleared easily.

Later in the garden, Gabriel was at my side, sharing his voltage and wisdom and love. "Love for Universal Spirit is what those in the Oneness have and desire."

# Chapter 14

# Negative Vortex

As I opened my heart to receiving everything the universe brought me as good, my life became magical; more of my positive intentions became reality. I enjoyed using my spiritual gifts and helping other people experience how the spiritual world around us worked. The separateness and fear I had always felt couldn't compete with knowing that I was an integral part of the universe and Universal Spirit; I was happier, calmer, less reactive, and more reflective.

My husband often said, "I really like the new you!"

I connected with nature easily by tuning into the joy, love, gratitude, wonder, and curiosity of the universe within me and feeling the aliveness of nature around me. Trees, plants, and water stretched toward the Oneness, their energy flowing upward and outward into me and the universe. When intuition pulled my attention toward the sun, its energy flowed into me also.

One day, my husband stood under the trees near our house with a finger placed to his lips and motioned for me to come near. Hearing a loud buzzing, I looked into the leaves and blossoms. Thousands of bees were sipping nectar!

I looked to the sky; feeling its joy, I said loudly, "Thank you."

As my gratitude reverberated through the universe, the sun came from behind a cloud to bless me with light until I went indoors.

The next time I visited my mom, I noticed the one-hundred-twenty-year-old cottonwood trees lining the driveway on the farm where I grew up were losing branches. I held one of them, feeling sad for it. "Thank you for always being part of my life."

Tree said, "I'm old and will return to the earth. All is good."

A few days later, in a biofield session, a friend said, "I want the energy of the large oak tree at my childhood home to join me today. Do you think it has a name?"

Holding her intention, I said to the tree, "Do you have a name?"

"I *am*."

Oak tree vibration filled the room. "I am part of the great 'I *am*.' I exist only in each present moment, as Universal Spirit exists; it *is*."

One day, I awoke groggy from a nap. An hour later, still

needing to clear my mind, I stepped outside to be grounded by the earth's energy. I hugged a tree. "Can you clear my mind?"

"Yes."

"Really?"

"Yes."

I leaned against the tree; energy moved through my body. "How will I know when you're done?"

"You'll know."

In a few moments, my energy flowed up and out with the tree's energy! The continual flow from foot to crown became lighter and stronger. Suddenly, I knew! I stepped away from the tree with gratitude.

One winter morning was warm and balmy; a change was coming. I turned my attention from the cat's purr to the universe, expecting to feel nature's joy or see swirls of Gabriel's presence. But today I heard one word. "Come."

It was the magnetism of the whole for all the parts—the yearning I had felt all my life but had never known where to look or what to do. Universal Spirit was calling me to express my own spirit fully so the whole could be all it could be.

Later, the full moon was covered with clouds when I peeked out the window, but soon the clouds slid away and the moon shone brightly over the garden. I soaked up its energy, then ran outside to enjoy it more. Strolling through the garden barefoot the next morning, I only felt my spirit body, not the physical; I was light flowing through light.

During a hypnosis session, my friend read my first questions for the Oneness. "Do all plants communicate with each other? Do plants communicate with animals? Or do they all just communicate with the biofield of nature?"

I sent my question into the Oneness and told my friend the response I heard. "When I talk to one tree, the tree doesn't communicate the information to the rest of nature, but all of nature feels my vibration as if I spoke to each one."

My friend said, "They're all 'I *am*.'"

Then she read the next question. "You want to know more about ley lines."

I asked the Oneness and felt its wisdom and energy swirling around me. "Ley lines are the power grid of the universe; they flow directly from the pure energy of Universal Spirit deep under the earth, then filter up and disperse at the earth's surface to fuel all the energy lines that run across the earth."

I said to the Oneness, "Can I feel how it works?"

In spirit, I was lifted up by the ley line energy; I flowed upward to where it accumulated high in the sky, then I was pulled backward into the energy deep under the earth.

I said to the Oneness, "How is the energy drawn below the earth?"

"Magnetism."

"Does it happen within the biofield of nature or in the biofield of Oneness? Or does it cycle through the unending energy beyond the Oneness?"

My spirit was in the ley line energy again, flowing through

the top of nature's field and into the biofield of Oneness, then it was drawn back into the deep pool of energy under the earth.

Days later, in meditation, I saw that all ley lines used to connect at ninety-degree angles. Man-made changes to earth and the lower voltage of the universe had altered—and continued to change—the flow of some ley lines; some vortexes became negative, having angles other than ninety degrees.

One day, knowing that ancestors in the waiting place liked to be near negative vortexes, I said to the universe, "Is there a negative vortex in my town?"

My dowsing rods opened wide for a yes.

"What direction is it?"

The rods pointed.

I held them over that area of the city map. "Show me the negative vortex."

I followed the rods down the block and around the corner from my home. "Is the vortex on the north or south of the street?"

I stepped onto private property; I could feel a ley line. "Show me the vortex."

One day, when I walked down that street, I felt a spirit being near me. Its vibration felt similar to Gabriel's, but didn't have the joy and love like angels in the Oneness.

I said, "Who are you?"

The earth-realm angel just watched me walk away. A minute later, as I entered my garden, the high-voltage love and joy of Gabriel greeted me. I said, "Do you have a word for me?"

He said, "I wanted you to know I was with you."

# Chapter 15

# Earth-Realm Angels

During hypnosis, I said to the Oneness, "How many kinds of angels are there?"

I felt two distinct vibrations around me and called them guardian angels and archangels. Guardian angels worked with people; archangels worked with other parts of the universe. Some of each kind existed on earth in the biofield of nature; both kinds were in the Oneness also.

I said to Universal Spirit, "Did earth-realm angels used to once live in the Oneness?"

"Yes, but they thought they would have more freedom and authority on earth, so they chose to leave the Oneness."

Intuition called me outdoors; I stood in the ley line, sensing into the spiritual world around me. Universal Spirit took me in a vision to a place without light that vibrated with sadness and smelled like stagnant wastewater. Many angels were there, grayscale like ancestors in the waiting place, but they had higher voltage than the ancestors.

I said, "But what about the angels who love you?"

"The angels in the Oneness are with me everywhere."

Suddenly, I could feel them surrounding me, brighter and stronger than ancestors in the Oneness, and vibrating with love and joy.

One day, in my garden, an angelic presence moved toward me. It said, "I want to cover you with my love."

Not feeling threatened or scared, I allowed it to spread over me, but I felt grayness, not light or love. "You're not from the Oneness; leave me now."

The earth-realm angel moved away from me and left the garden.

One morning, during meditation, I said to Universal Spirit, "I want to know more about how the universe works."

Just then a spirit entered the room with a cool breeze. He said, "I've been sent to answer your questions."

All my other questions in meditation had been answered directly either by Universal Spirit through words or vision, or by intuition giving me a strong inner knowing. "Are you one with Universal Spirit?"

The being remained silent; I didn't feel the love and joy of the Oneness in its energy. Only wanting wisdom and knowledge from the highest source, I remembered the cool breeze. "You need to leave."

It disappeared.

One day, an earth-realm angel came to my garden from the direction of the negative vortex; his vibration was asking me to help him transition. Uncertain, I ignored him. But as I entered my house, I was thrown into an emotional tizzy, wanting to curl up and cry. The gray angel was in the room.

I said to Universal Spirit, "Can earth-realm angels transition back into the Oneness?"

"You know the answer; you desire the restoration of all things."

"Is it safe for me to help them transition, or can they keep me from being deeply connected with you?"

"They pretend to have power and authority to be able to control people, but if they don't want to go to the Oneness, they have to leave when you tell them. Other earth-realm angels will be angry if one of them transitions, but if you hold the intention that they cannot harm you or your family, they can't."

I said to angels and ancestors in the Oneness, "Is it okay with you if earth-realm angels return to the Oneness?"

Their voices sounded in unison all across the room. "Yes!"

Holding the intention that I was protected, I said to the earth-realm angel, "If you are ready to be in the Oneness, you can go now."

I felt a cool breeze as the angel moved past me and stood in the vortex. He was equally male and female. He moved like an ancestor, was two or three times bigger, and much taller than the ceiling. His transition felt like friction that moved slowly from my head to my feet as he entered the other biofield. It used more of my energy, and took longer than ancestors did.

I said, "If there's any other angel ready to transition today, please come now."

Four came; each was twelve feet tall. The vibration was intense, and again, the transition took longer than for an ancestor; I was worn out. In a second, the restored angels came from the Oneness and hugged me with gratitude, then returned to the Oneness.

When ancestors enter the Oneness, they look around at everything with awe and wonder, as if seeing something unfamiliar to them. But the newly transitioned angels were excitedly remembering things they used to know about the universe before they left.

I said, "Dad, how do you feel about angels returning to the Oneness?"

He enveloped me with his love and joy for the universe, including for the new additions in the Oneness.

Often, ancestors from generations long ago who were ready to transition came to my home after dark. One evening after ancestors had transitioned, I said, "If any angels are ready, you are welcome to come now."

"We're ready."

As the three angels transitioned, their energy felt frayed, like a mild electric shock or electromagnetic damage, just as the outer edges of the Restoration Group had the first time I tuned them. Afterward, I wanted to sit down and rest, but one who was much larger than the others entered the room. I said to the archangel, "Transition now or leave. You can't stay."

He joined the Oneness, returned to thank me, and left again.

In my next hypnosis session, I said to Universal Spirit, "Why do earth-realm angels have a more intense and longer transition? Ancestors use very little of my energy, but when an earth-realm angel transitions, my whole body vibrates slowly from head to foot as if I'm the angel entering the Oneness."

"Their frequency is different than ancestors, and their voltage is higher because they are bigger, but also because their knowledge is greater."

"Why do they speak with an authority that the ancestors don't speak with?"

"They know more. They know who they are, what happens in the spirit world, and what has happened in the universe. Ancestors don't have this knowledge until they get to the Oneness."

A friend who came for a tuning was upset, expecting to lose her job because she wouldn't take a required vaccine; my fork pulled away dense energy that wasn't hers. One of her ancestors in the room said, "I lied so much during my life and brought negativity to others; I took away their positive energy with my lies."

As I continued clearing the ancestor's energy, he spoke again. "I really want to join the Oneness, but I don't think I can because of all my lies."

I said, "Yes, you can! We're clearing your regret for your lies, and you can join the Oneness today."

After his pocket of energy cleared, I was stuck in dissonance at the outer edge of my friend's ancestral field; again I felt dense energy blocking my work. An earth-realm angel stood outside my house as if holding on to the shirttail of the ancestral field, attaching his controlling attitude to my friend and the ancestor who wanted to be free.

Intuition said the angel represented all the spiritual energies, hierarchy, and lies that were keeping my friend and her ancestors from knowing they were made of Universal Spirit. I said to the angel, "You have no right to hold them! Leave."

The energy cleared quickly as the angel left.

As I worked with a friend who wanted to increase her awareness of a constant connection with Universal Spirit, an earth-realm angel appeared next to me. The forceful tone of his words and his vibration of anger and manipulation were meant as a threat. "Why are you doing this?"

Obviously, he didn't want the Oneness, and he didn't want my friend to desire it either. So I jumped across the room to stand in the vortex for higher voltage, and faced him. "We have the right to know we are made of Universal Spirit and to choose to live as spirit beings."

# Chapter 16

# Hierarchy

A few weeks later my hypnotist read my questions for the Oneness. "Does hierarchy exist within the waiting place? Earth-realm angels don't have power over us, but can an ancestor prevent others from transitioning?"

As I used all my senses to feel into the Oneness, the answer came quickly. "Ancestors who desire hierarchy during their lives desire hierarchy when they die. Just as with living people, some ancestors like to rule over others and exert their influence through control and manipulation; other ancestors feel powerless or want to be ruled over. But there's no hierarchy by the universe—only by individuals. They only have the power you give them."

Later, in meditation, I said to Universal Spirit, "How can I help ancestors realize their power? And how can I help the living know they have spiritual rights?"

The next day, as I breathed in from above my head and into my heart, pockets of stuck energy cleared at each chakra as I exhaled. That's how! Spiritual rights were represented in every chakra!

I tuned myself to activate and amplify my awareness of my spiritual rights. I invited my ancestors in the waiting place to activate their rights too. And I invited those in the Oneness too, even though they knew their rights, because their intention could help empower the rest of us. Gabriel stood across the table guiding my words and actions.

Striking a fork to tune the crown chakra at the top of my head, I said, "We have the right to live in the present moment. We have the right to know we are made of Universal Spirit and the right to receive our spiritual rights."

When dissonance cleared, I held the fork at the third eye of the hologram. "We have the right to use our whole minds in harmony and hear our spirits above the chatter of the mind. We have the right to receive the wisdom and knowledge of the universe."

At the throat, I said, "We have the right to express our spirits boldly above the confusion of the hierarchical mindset. We have the right to hear Universal Spirit speak to us and to receive the clarity we need to stand in those truths."

I struck the fork at the heart. "We have the right to know the love that Universal Spirit has for us, to know we are that love, and to receive that love."

Moving to the solar plexus, I said, "We have the right to claim our authority and power over the mindset of lack, fear, and control. We have the right to receive the power and support of the universe."

Next was the sacral chakra. "We have the right to create our own lives by listening to our spirits. We have the right to know our value as an integral part of Universal Spirit."

I activated my fork at the tailbone, the root. "We have the right to know that because all things are made of Universal Spirit, all things are good; we are always safe because we can never be separated from Universal Spirit. We have the right to live in the mindset of Universal Spirit—the mindset of abundance."

The chakra at the bottom of the hologram's central channel was at the ankles instead of a foot below the feet; my ancestors and I still often reacted in fight or flight, which reduced the voltage and size of our biofields. I moved it lower and grounded us to the energy deep below the earth. "We have the right to know we are a connection between earth and sky. We have the right to connect with Universal Spirit."

The chakra at the top of the channel needed to be moved out further too. "We have the right to know we are a connection between the physical and spiritual. We have the right to connect with the Oneness."

Crystals placed on each of the energy centers of the hologram amplified energy flow in the channel and around the outer edge of the biofield. "We have the right to receive the helpful frequencies of the universe. We have the right to protect our spirits and bodies from harmful frequencies used by hierarchical minds."

Tuning the chakra fifteen to twenty inches below my hologram's feet, I said, "We have the right to know we are spirit beings—individualized portions of Universal Spirit—and that our spirits are designed to lead the mind."

Life purpose energy was fifteen to twenty inches above the head. "We have the right to receive everything the universe brings as good instead of reacting in fight, flight, or freeze. We have the right to recognize when we are at this choice point."

Forty inches above the crown, was our soul's purpose. "We have the right to choose to live as spirit beings. We have the right to choose to be all our spirits desire to be."

The chakra just inside the hologram's outer edge was part of the light waves constantly connecting us to Universal Spirit, condensing to form the connective tissues in our bodies. "We have the right to give and receive in harmony with the abundance of the universe."

And last, I tuned the energy center just outside the hologram's outer edge. "We have the right to know we came from the Oneness and will return to the Oneness. We have the right to fully express the desires of our spirits."

I made swirls of figure eights throughout the biofield. "We have the right to be masters of all our energy. We have the right to use the energy of the universe with every breath we take."

From the solar plexus, I claimed our power. "We have the right to know and claim our spiritual rights for the highest good of all."

Completing the session, I said, "We have the right to feel safe and secure in our rights. We give thanks, and so it is."

After my ancestors transitioned, my guardian angel said, "I'm with you to protect your spiritual rights—if you want them."

I said, "Since every person is made of Universal Spirit, each person's spirit always wants their spiritual rights, don't they?"

"Most people have forgotten that they are spirit beings and don't know they have these rights."

From then on, when I tuned the Restoration Group, I included the universe and myself in the hologram and tuned our spiritual rights, broadcasting knowledge of those rights through the light waves to every being in the universe.

During one friend's session, the pendulum showed me to clear stuck energy at the throat chakra. Her father, who had died several years earlier, came to transition. As I worked in her father's memories within her ancestral field, I heard him as a child yelling, "No! No!"

He had been in a spiritual battle, unable to speak his truth during much of his life. Even now something was trying to hold him back from transitioning. I held my tuning forks in the stuck energy of his struggle and said to him, "If you want your spiritual rights, repeat them after me."

One at a time he claimed his rights, and soon he was free.

In a later session, this same friend wanted to remove blocks within her that would help her ancestors transition. As my tuning fork pulled away negative energy that didn't belong to her, the energy was dense, the fork dissonant. She said, "I haven't been feeling safe this week, but I don't know why."

I used the pendulum. "We're going to work in subconscious thought today."

My fork vibrated at the outer edge of her ancestral field. "A lot of your ancestors are outside my house, but they're not ready to transition. They're divided into two groups; both groups are low voltage and are standing in darkness, as if it's the middle of the night, dressed in clothing from many eras. Both groups are angry. Those on the right don't want you to release the thought patterns that have kept you from moving forward in your life, and they don't want the ancestors on the left to know that they can join the Oneness. The group on the left is hesitant; they don't know what they want. They're used to following orders and letting others decide things for them."

I stepped quietly across the room. "The energy feels weird, like I'm walking through a house on tiptoe trying not to wake people who are sleeping."

Suddenly, a whirlwind of energy pushed me through the rest of the field; I returned with a different fork. "The energy has shifted a bit; the ancestors are still gathered outside the window, and the ones on my right are still angry. But the anger of the ancestors on the left is starting to crumble; an independent thought is now part of their vibration. It feels like they're saying, 'I think maybe I might want to transition sometime.'"

Two months later, my friend was back for another session; ancestors stood outside the window again. Of the ancestors from the group on the left—those who were being controlled—twelve were ready to transition, but they represented all her ancestors who wanted to help her step into her power and be all she is meant to be. One hundred forty-four transitioned.

After the session, she said, "I've worked with mediums and did other ancestral clearing before coming to you, but I've never had any contact with ancestors on my father's side."

"We held the intention of spiritual restoration of your original blueprint and that of your ancestors. The spirits of our ancestors yearn for restoration, but like us, their minds often can't hear their spirits because they live in their old patterns of fear and control.

"Your ancestors in both groups seemed to be involved with some kind of hierarchical leadership within the waiting place. Hierarchy has two sides; those who like to be ruled over and those who like to rule over others. But those wanting control only have the power we give them; the universe works on free choice."

Another two months passed; the same friend came to her session feeling a heavy presence of ancestors from the hierarchy on her father's side. Sadness filled her ancestral edge; my spirit pleaded with them to listen to their spirit and join the Oneness.

I kept her informed as I worked. "I've cleared pockets of stuck energy at ages ten, fifteen, twenty, thirty, forty, fifty, sixty, and seventy. It felt like initiation rites into the hierarchy: Ancestors taught their descendents to die to awareness of their spirit and trained them to lead the hierarchy in the waiting place. Members in the waiting place met the living at the moment of death and escorted them to the group so they didn't change their minds."

Energy trapped at their deaths was full of regrets and sadness too. In my friend's personal field, I cleared ancestral influence on both sides of her body. Fifty-five from the hierarchy transitioned.

A few days later, she sent a text. "Yesterday, I couldn't breathe or catch my breath; I was afraid I'd have to call for help. I felt I was battling for my breath, fighting with good, beautiful, positive thoughts against something dark that was taking my breath . . ."

At her next session, eighteen ancestors from the hierarchical leadership transitioned with gratitude. They had a message for her. "We're looking forward to the joy and abundance of the Oneness; all we have ever known is the lack and control of hierarchy."

The following week, she was still coughing, though she didn't have a cold. Immediately, I tuned her throat and sacral chakras, then her heart. I said, "Say 'yah' three times; it's the sound of an open heart."

Her energy felt freer; her father and grandfather came from the Oneness to acknowledge her intention to help their ancestors. Intuition prompted me. "Your ancestors were trained in hierarchy from a young age and were met at death to be taken into the hierarchy of the waiting place; they never fully expressed their own truth or love."

Her ancestral field was full of ancestors who followed the fork to the vortex. As she gave a blessing, I heard a roar from where the ancestors were gathered. They reached out their arms with love and gratitude and spoke in unison. "Yah."

# Chapter 17

# Other Energies

One day, the emotional energy that had been released during a friend's biofield session hung around me. I claimed my rights, using intention and a tuning fork to pull the energy away from my body and send it out of my house. Balance and harmony returned.

A few days later, my mother welcomed me as I walked through her garden; her hug conveyed her love and gladness to see me. But as I stepped into her house, a wave of negative energy flooded toward me: vibrations of the sadness and fear I'd felt while growing up. But it wasn't my energy; I didn't feel that way anymore. Silently I said, "No. I don't receive this energy."

I sent the house love and gratitude. My parents had always loved and supported me while I grew up; I just hadn't loved myself. As the negative energy dissipated, I embraced the sadness and fear I'd felt during anorexia; everything in my life had helped me be where I am now.

Later as I visited my sister, vibrations of hurt and anger her house had absorbed during a heated argument years ago tried to envelop me. I only felt love toward her now. "No. These feelings aren't mine."

I welcomed the home's energy and all the old stories of my life, transmuting the vibrations into love.

Weeks later at mom's house again, as I connected to Universal Spirit deep under the earth, my head turned quickly to the northwest tracing the flow of a ley line. A positive vortex was within half a mile!

As I walked the road bordering her farm, two ancestors came to my side wanting to transition. I held the intention for them to transition from the vortex near us; my eyes followed their energy into a grove of trees one hundred yards long and half that wide.

Without dowsing rods or a pendulum, a tingle in my arm served as a guide. I walked through a grass-covered field, then entered the grove of trees, stopping every few steps to feel the energy. I crossed a dry creek bed, stepped over dead tree trunks, and pushed through overgrowth. The tingle grew stronger; I was in the positive vortex.

Moving past the vortex, I sensed another vortex nearby and followed the ley line northward through the grove, still using my arm as a guide. The energy was strong among a cluster of huge trees; decaying trunks and broken branches littered the ground. I took steps several feet in every direction but couldn't find the vortex.

Unsettling dreams interrupted my sleep that night; by morning I was tired and out of sorts. Though I willingly helped prepare the holiday meal, I pushed myself to keep up with kitchen chores and struggled with my old thought pattern of anger toward others. "They don't love me or they wouldn't make me do all this work; I must be unworthy of their love—I'm not good enough."

The next morning, still unhappy and out of alignment with my spirit and my husband, I received a biofield session. "I think energies from a negative vortex may have attached to me."

The practitioner said, "Your energy won't ground."

With intuition guiding, she used her forks to pull away negative energy that wasn't mine. Intense resistance in a deep pocket finally released with my tears; soon I was smiling, at peace again.

She said, "We have Carla back now!"

To protect myself from other negative energies, I connected daily with Universal Spirit, breathing in its sparkling purple energy from deep under the earth—the color of royalty, to remind me of my true worth as a part of Universal Spirit. It filled my biofield, home, and garden with power and light. Then I inhaled the descending spiral of energy from ancestors and angels in the Oneness, drawing in the love and support of those who are always full of Universal Spirit.

I breathed from the deep energy again, this time welcoming

the wisdom and strength of Universal Spirit in the ascending sacred spiral flow of life. Then I inhaled all the resources of the universe around me to remind myself the universe was always working in my favor, and I always had all I needed. And then I breathed in the positive ley line vortex energy to empower me to create the life I wanted.

As I ended the meditation, I said, "I claim Universal Spirit's protection today from all negative and low-voltage energies I don't need to experience, and from the hierarchical mindset of lack, fear, and control within me and in the world."

The next time I received a biofield session, the practitioner said, "Your stuck energy doesn't want to release; I'll pull away any negative energy that isn't yours."

A few minutes later, she said, "Now the forks are stuck in a large pocket of energy that has formed a shackle around your ankle!"

As she worked to clear the shackle, my body reacted by scrunching up my right eye and ear; energy shifted, and unmet needs from earlier in my life filled my heart. I squirmed, my right foot trying to drag my left leg across the massage table. As the stuck energy cleared, my ankle longed for love, so I sent it all my love. After the practitioner used several different tuning forks, burned sage, and wiped my hologram clean of any debris, the shackle was gone. The next day, I noticed several times that I flowed easily when unexpected changes interrupted my routine instead of reacting in my usual pattern; over the next few days, more patterns changed.

During my next hypnotism, my friend read from my list

of questions for the Oneness. "What was the shackle, or what did it symbolize?"

I looked at my ankle; the shackle was definitely gone. I waited for wisdom. "The shackle was generations of ancestors with the mindset of lack. Now I'm free!"

Angels in the Oneness said, "Move forward with the authority, knowledge, and wisdom you have, and know that Universal Spirit is always with you."

My friend said, "Do you believe Universal Spirit is always with you?"

"Yes! We're made of Universal Spirit. Our minds forget this truth, think we lack, and react in fear or control."

A few days after the session, negative thoughts kept coming to my mind—old stories I'd been shackled in. I reinforced my restored energy flow by focusing on where I felt the lack and fear in my body and filling it with love.

But other thoughts felt like negative energy from another source. I inhaled the power of Universal Spirit and was filled with love and gratitude for all the energy available to me at all times. I held up my hand as a stop sign. "Any energy that is not mine must leave!"

Then I held out my other hand, palm up to receive. "I call back all my energy that has been pulled away by negative energies."

Negative thoughts cleared but later returned; after the third rebuttal, they left me alone.

One day, I was receiving a biofield session; six time zones

away, the practitioner struck her forks as thunder sounded over our Zoom connection and rain poured onto her house. She said, "Let's wait a few minutes; storms like this aren't common here."

I said, "I like to give tunings during rain because there's so much extra energy in the air. I'd love it if you would tune me during the storm."

As she worked, a large range of emotions flashed through me: fear, severe powerlessness, sadness, anger. Most were very intense; some came with visions. Halfway through the session, the tuning forks found my adrenal energy in the biofield; both of us felt my energy change suddenly, becoming very cold and hard. She said, "I need to use different forks."

We lost internet connection, but from energy and emotional fluctuations, I knew she was still working. In a vision, I was the ancient grandfather who had held my spirit's intentions; he was being tortured. As his pain cleared, the session ended.

Once the practitioner's electricity was restored, we compared notes. I said, "In nearly every hypnosis session, when I'm at my deepest point of emotional and spiritual connection, the phone disconnects."

She said, "My husband was in the room below. He heard a blood-curdling scream coming from where I was working. As he prayed for God to put a stop to whatever was not as it should be, lightning struck our house. He opened the front door to check for damage just as a red energy form darted across the yard. There were several items plugged into a power strip, but the internet router was the only thing damaged."

I said, "My emotions were intense during the session, and at the end I was suddenly cold—much colder than when ancestors come to transition. An earth-realm archangel was waiting to transition; he must have flowed through me to get to the vortex."

The next day, as I tuned a child, something blocked the ascending flow of her central channel, but it wasn't her stuck energy. I said to the universe, "Is this an ancestor? Maybe a sibling who died in her mother's womb is attached to her?"

No answer.

"Is it some kind of negative being?"

No answer again.

"Is it a type of negative energy?"

Yes. It was purposefully blocking her energy flow and didn't budge. I claimed her spiritual rights and said to the energy, "You must leave."

With firm insistence and many strikes of the tuning fork, it left her body but was still in her field; I dragged it into the vortex to be transmuted.

With the ascending flow now free, I grounded her descending energy flow to the Oneness. Wooosh! Ancestors from the Oneness joined her with gladness and gratitude, as if it had been a long time since they had been able to fully connect with her.

Adding sound waves to intention, I claimed the light and sacred geometry of Universal Spirit and the power of the positive vortex to fill any void left when the energy receded and to protect her from all negative or low-voltage energy for the rest of the day.

# Chapter 18

# Blame

Hoping to experience what life would be like if my original divine blueprint was restored, I listened to new ideas and meditations for personal growth and wrote down any of the words or phrases used that were different from words I had already cleared for. I focused my attention, intention, and breath on releasing the stuck energy of old thought patterns and misconceptions that were associated with those words.

After a day of much personal clearing, I woke at 3:30 a.m. as Gabriel poured wisdom and knowledge into my crown chakra. I had no idea what wisdom I had been given, but a few days later in meditation, energy stirred within me. "What's happening?"

Universal Spirit said, "The information from the other night is being activated."

I rested my hands on my legs, palms up. "I receive all."

My ancestors from the Oneness gathered around; one grandfather placed his hand on my shoulder.

I said, "Thank you, all of you."

Dad hugged me. "Love my family."

"I do."

A few days later, as I received a biofield session, the practitioner said, "I'm stuck in energy from when you were fifty-two."

"I was asked to resign from a difficult job; it was a painful time for me. It's never come up during a tuning before; I must have processed it enough that it's ready to clear."

The following day, I was emotional, and old thought patterns triggered easily; I tuned myself to help bring balance and harmony.

As I finished a friend's biofield session, she said, "I've been learning about the importance of family lines; it's made me take more time to be with my parents and learn about what interests them. My dad has a big garden, so I've started asking about it and listening to him talk. It's created more of a bond between us; I feel more connection."

"My dad's in the Oneness; twice in the past few months he's come to me and said, 'Love my family.' Each time, I said, 'I do love them.' But part of my vibration must be saying I don't."

I hesitated to share more. "Nine years ago, I had a big disagreement with my family; a few months later, Dad died, and some of them blamed me for his death. I had a stressful job, and by the first anniversary of his death, my mind wasn't working right."

My friend said, "That's a lot of negative energy to hold on to. Have you forgiven them?"

"Yes."

But my eyes blurred with tears; all at once, I felt so tired.

"Have you really? It takes a lot to fully forgive something like that. Do you blame yourself?"

I wiped my eyes again.

The next morning, knowing my body would tell me if I had blocks in my energy flow for blame, shame, and forgiveness, I tested my muscle strength while naming each emotion out loud. My muscles had weakness for all three; I used Yoga exercises with positive affirmations to help release the blocks.

In a vision during meditation, I stood in the Oneness; my ancestors gathered in front of me. We exchanged wisdom; I received and gave, then received and asked for more. "How can I clear myself of this blame and forgiveness?"

Dad stepped forward from the ancestors and took me in a vision within the first vision. "Do you remember summer evenings as you were growing up? When the temperature cooled, our family often walked down the driveway, stepped into a plowed field, and looked for seashells or arrowheads. Many times we found parts of seashells, sometimes half shells. But once in a great while, we found an arrowhead, and considered it a real prize."

As he spoke, I caught the sweet scent of flowers in bloom; warm sand squeezed between my bare toes as we walked down the road, the evening sun still hot enough to make sweat beads on my forehead. I felt the safety of being with my family, the hardness of dirt clods against my feet as I walked in the field, and the joy of finding a full arrowhead one time. "I remember."

"As you look inside yourself, the shells are emotions you will release as you find them. And in time you will find an arrowhead—your deepest pain ready to be cleared—and you will rejoice."

Blinded by tears, I tried to imagine, as real as in life, hugging my dad.

Dad said, "I love you."

Memories of being with him, just the two of us, filled my heart. "I love you too."

"Those times are special to me too."

"You remember those times, even now, in the Oneness?"

"Of course."

Later that week, I tuned myself to help forgive myself and others. The pendulum showed I needed to work at my third eye. Why is it telling me to work here? The third eye's about worry and regret, not forgiveness! As I cleared those old patterns, the forks found the difficult years of Dad's death and losing my job. Did all the worry and regret from those experiences need to be cleared before I could forgive?

My husband was building a metal garden fence for me; I picked up a small section. He said, "You're always so competitive, trying to keep one step ahead of me!"

He had commented on my competitiveness at other times, and I had scoffed; today I accepted it with gratitude. "I'm not trying to outdo you; I just like to help. But I think it's from my old story of wanting approval and trying to prove that I'm good enough."

Dad had been a bricklayer; he expected me to think ahead and have cement and bricks ready when I helped him. I tried hard, wanting his approval and to show I was good enough. Even when I had my own family and he helped me with home improvements, I had always tried to do my best to please him.

I had wanted Mom's approval too, and often I still did, as if my own opinions didn't matter. Had I held on to the blame surrounding Dad's death because I felt my own approval was not enough?

As I received a biofield session to help clear myself from blaming others and blaming myself, the pendulum indicated a need to clear energy at my heart chakra. The practitioner activated her tuning forks. "There's a lot of stuck energy right here at gestation."

"It's my birth story; I feared rejection and separation, wanted approval, and blamed myself."

"Now I'm stuck in your early teens."

"Anorexia's a slow suicide. I felt sad, lonely, and not good enough most of the time."

"You're eighteen."

"Anorexia was worse then."

She continued her work. "Now you're twenty-three."

"I was in an abusive marriage."

"Now you're twenty-eight. Did your husband have addictions?"

"Yeah. He blamed me for everything, and I believed him."

"In this pocket, you're thirty-one."

"My second marriage failed. I blamed myself for ruining my life and my children's future."

"Now you're forty-three."

"My boys were having difficult junior high years; I wasn't able to take away the pain my mistakes had caused them."

The practitioner was only a few inches away from my body. "This energy is heavy; it's from eight or nine years ago."

"When I was growing up, my father wanted to attend the church he grew up in, but Mom wanted to raise her children in a local church. Some of Dad's older brothers pressured him, causing animosity between families. My siblings and I felt this animosity frequently and sided with Mom. Not wanting to risk losing his wife and children, Dad stayed in the local church."

I gave in to the memory I had tried to avoid for nine years. "Dad had dementia. Getting older brought back his desire to attend his family's church, but he didn't drive more than a few miles from home anymore. The brothers who had pressured Dad had died, and my siblings and I had our own families.

"As an administrator of an adult care home, protecting the rights of the elderly every day, I wanted Dad to be able to follow his heart's desire if he wanted to. When I offered to drive him to church, he said, 'I think I can do it now if at least one of my children accepts me.'

"When he came to visit me at my office a few days later, his blue eyes were shining so bright; I had only seen them dulled for a long time.

"But after fifty years of animosity, my family was angry. When he died a few months later, some of them blamed me. Grief added to my stressful job; a year later, I hated myself for getting fired."

As the pocket of energy cleared, my friend said, "I think you were very strong to help your father. You acted in love; there is no blame."

Later, I said to my husband, "Dad knew his mind wasn't working right, yet he drove himself to church that night during a snowstorm. Dementia had limited his quality of life; he probably felt death was a blessing.

"After a year of grief, blame, and job stress, my mind wasn't working right; I watched myself making poor decisions but was unable to stop. Being fired was painful, but leaving the job was a relief.

"Maybe at times when our minds can't take care of us, our spirits take charge. Maybe when situations seem to bring bad things into our lives, it's really our spirits working in our favor. If so, at those times, there would be no offense, so there would be no blame."

He said, "If we're being blamed by others, it's not helpful to think we're not blamed. And if we only think we're being blamed but aren't, that's not helpful either. How can we know where reality stops and only our perception remains?"

"If our minds always received everything as being for our highest good, there would never be an offense or blame, real or perceived."

Two weeks later, my biofield practitioner said, "I think we should do another session to clear for blame. Have you asked your dad if he blamed you for his death?"

"No! Why would he blame me? I was helping him."

But after the session I called through the universe, "Dad, I really want to talk to you. Please come."

His attention was present.

"Did you blame me for your death?"

His vibration was only love, but I swallowed hard; part of me still blamed me.

# Chapter 19

# Conscious Connection

In springtime, we drove through a large city; most trees were surrounded by concrete.

Universal Spirit said, "Hear my voice."

My eyes were overwhelmed with the sadness of nature. "Why are they so sad?"

"You know."

I listened again; the trees could not feel Universal Spirit the way they wanted to; the city had low spiritual voltage. Electromagnetic interference was high, and most people had forgotten how to connect with nature or Universal Spirit every day; their minds turned as fast as the tires on their cars.

Focusing my mind to be the spiritual connection between the trees and Universal Spirit, my pulse surged up and down in my central channel, then stopped; the sadness of nature poured through me again.

Every tree said, "Why don't they want me? I'm here for them."

But the words were Universal Spirit; the whole was yearning for all the parts.

As I continued to focus, sadness released, and their connection to the Oneness was restored; others in the city were consciously being the connection between nature and Universal Spirit too, just not enough for continual connection.

Home again, I held a tree outside our front door. Tree said, "Learn all you can so you can help us."

"What do you mean?"

Tree spoke again. "Things will get worse before they get better. You can help us."

"What do I need to learn? What's going to happen?"

"We'll help you too."

What did I need to learn? How could I help the trees or the universe? I said to Universal Spirit, "Please bring me what I need to help the trees and everyone else during the times coming!"

My plea flowed through the universe. The Oneness was near. Dad stood on my right with the ancestor who had held my spirit intentions; Grandpa was on my left with the ancient grandfather who knew about the sky clock. Gabriel placed information into my central channel to be revealed to my conscious mind at the right time.

That evening, the friend who had told me about the Egyptian hieroglyphics sent a video link. "You'll understand this in your own knowledge."

A sentence halfway through the video spoke to me. Because all trees were connected through the earth, they broadcast our intentions to the universe millions of times through their leaves!

I ran outside and held the tree again, standing as close as I could, hands and forehead touching its trunk. I said with all my heart, "Please broadcast my love for Universal Spirit, the universe, and nature, and broadcast my desire to flow with the abundance of the universe."

Strong tree energy pulled my own energy upward and out through its leaves and into the universe for a few powerful seconds.

The tree said, "It is done."

"How often do I need to broadcast my intentions?"

"Anytime a desire from your spirit needs to be broadcast."

A few days later, I emailed my hypnotist a new list of questions. She helped me settle into awareness of being part of the Oneness, then read a question. "The trees told you, 'Things will get bad before they get better.' How can you help nature prepare for and thrive during those difficult times?"

I felt into the Oneness and told my friend what they said. "We can send our intention of restoration, our positive voltage, and our love for nature through the trees into the universe! Electromagnetic frequencies—and people's intentions of control—interfere with nature's ability to receive the helpful vibrations it needs from the universe."

After the session, I discussed ideas with my guardian angel. "I know we have the power of Universal Spirit within us; when we choose to live as spirit beings instead of just the physical, our voltage is very great and will really help nature. But is there more I need to know?"

Gabriel said, "The positive voltage of your intention will change harmful frequencies to helpful ones. Send it through the trees."

The love and gratitude of nature helped me form an intention. The next morning, rain energy filled my garden, amplifying those intentions as I held a tree. "Please send the intention that my energy will transmute harmful frequencies into the next higher helpful frequency."

My intention flowed with tree energy through the leaves and into the sky, but it didn't feel as powerful as I thought it would. I said, "What can I do to help my intention be more effective?"

Tree said, "It doesn't have to be the next highest frequency; just transmute it into helpful ones."

Gabriel said, "After focusing on sending the intention through the tree, place your attention in the sky, as if you are actually seeing harmful frequencies changed into helpful ones."

I held the tree and my intention again, seeing in my mind the power of the universe transmuting energy in the sky. Power surged through me! When it subsided, I stepped away from the tree, still full of energy. Maybe I could make the intention even stronger by organizing a group of people to hold the trees at the same time; we could recharge ourselves as we helped the universe! Tears filled my eyes; I said to Universal Spirit, "Thank you so much."

I hugged the tree, wondering what it thought.

It said, "We love you. You are sunshine for our soul. Thank you for all your help."

# Chapter 20

# Abundance and Lack

In meditation, Universal Spirit said, "Please come with me."

"I always want to be with you."

Universal Spirit swirled into my crown and filled me. "I am you; we are one."

I smiled with all my heart. "Yes, we are! Thank you! But why does my mind take over, fearing I'm not enough or don't have enough? Why can't I always listen to my spirit, knowing I have great abundance?"

"The mind doesn't have to be in charge; people used to know they were spirit and taught their children how to live as spirit, but the knowledge was lost."

Universal Spirit took me in a vision to a time before hierarchical thoughts of fear and control ruled the world; many ancestors—living and dead—held the spirit's intentions for their descendents from before their descendents were conceived until they joined the Oneness. All generations knew they were spirit beings and chose for their spirits to be in charge. They knew they had access to the abundance of the universe, knew they were free to pursue their own desires, and always felt safe and valued. They taught every generation how to live in alignment with their spirit and how to live in tune with the energy flow of the universe. They encouraged each other to follow their own spirit's desires.

The frequency emitted by the giant trees used to reset the pathway of electrical flow in each person daily, if they wanted it; at that time, most people did. The living vibrated with the love, joy, and gratitude of the universe because they were connected with Universal Spirit and their ancestors in the Oneness. They enjoyed having a physical body as long as they wanted to, then returned to the Oneness.

But the people who didn't have the vibration of the universe hid this wisdom and knowledge; generations forgot they were spirit, the giant trees were cut down, the mindset of lack flourished, and the waiting place became their only afterlife.

"But why did you design our minds to be able to take charge over our spirit?"

"You have to choose to listen to your spirit by your own free will. Everyone is free to choose for themselves."

"But what about people who choose to harm or take advantage of others? They don't choose to live by spirit, and they don't help others live by spirit."

"You have free will, and they do also, because you exist as me, and I am all things."

"But I didn't have a choice over how my mother felt when she found she was pregnant again. When I was three, I didn't have a choice over what the man did to me; he was bigger and stronger than I was."

Universal Spirit took me in a vision again. "This was how the world was."

"I don't see anything, but I feel a low vibration of anxiousness or impatience."

"Exactly. That's how hierarchy in your mind begins. Feeling that you lack and then reacting—not thinking, not breathing, choosing to resist what is."

For most of my life, I had feared for my safety, thought I was unworthy, and blamed myself, or felt powerless and blamed others. I had chosen to feel like a victim; reacting in fear had brought the worry and stress of trying to protect myself and my resources. I hadn't known that I was as abundant as the universe, or that I could have that abundance.

I breathed in an abundance of love, joy, gratitude, wisdom, and knowledge. I breathed in everything my spirit desired, including self-love, self-worth, and self-approval. I felt loved. I felt gratitude for my love. And I was filled with joy, knowing that my spirit is always one with Universal Spirit. Everything I needed was within me; I am what everything is made of.

I scanned my body and sent love to stuck emotions that were blocking me from receiving all things from the universe.

Energy moved inside me, swirling, changing. I said to Universal Spirit, "What are you doing?"

"Restoring you."

My solar plexus flashed into my mind's eye, burning red, orange, and yellow as it radiated through me and throughout the universe.

After receiving several tunings over a few weeks, I could feel energy circuits being restored. One day in meditation, energy flowed forcefully into the center of my brain, as if it were going to pop through my crown and allow me to experience another realm, and then it subsided. Three times over the following days, the energy pulsed at my crown, then subsided.

I said to Universal Spirit, "What's happening?"

Swirling energy streamed into my heart chakra; I felt completely loved.

Universal Spirit said, "I'm always with you; in every breath you take, I am here."

Energy flowed into my third eye; again I had the feeling of almost breaking into another realm, but calmness opened inside me. Bluish green energy swirled around me in a big hug.

Universal Spirit said, "It's like the tree said; all is good. Soon you'll know what's happening inside you."

All things are good at all times, for all parts are the whole! Universal Spirit flowed in waves around me and in a column up to the Oneness; the universe sparkled with the energy of every resource I would ever need, shimmering and flowing until the perfect timing to coalesce into physical reality.

I said, "All I want is you; I want to know you."

Universal Spirit said, "I am all. You have all."

A few days later, I placed my hands on a tree, feeling its energy. "Do you have a word for me?"

The tree said, "Look up."

I saw sky and clouds through the branches.

"All of it is yours."

I breathed in the sky, clouds, and everything the universe had for me; I breathed in love in great abundance. Then I breathed in an abundance of money. But I didn't feel it.

I said an affirmation. "I'm worthy of all the money I'll ever need."

But I felt angry; when I was three, the man had given me a dime and said, "Don't tell anyone or you're a bad girl."

I didn't tell anyone; my mind had buried it to protect me. But my subconscious felt that money was bad, and because I had received his money, I was bad.

All at once, I realized the man had given me the money to make himself feel better. It had nothing to do with me! Money was not bad, and receiving it didn't make me bad; I was worthy of receiving money just because I am. I am abundance; all the energy of the universe is available to me in every breath!

My vibration had asked the universe for what I needed with every exhale; my fear of not having or being enough had only brought more lack.

Although my spirit's intention had always been to restore the original abundance of my biofield and body, my mind had feared lack for sixty years. As I learned to live as a spirit being and listen to my spirit, I became more relaxed and positive, happier and freer. And the universe felt these positive vibrations and returned more of it to me.

But when warning lights on the dash of our old car flashed, and the engine surged, my old hamster wheel of worry was back with vengeance. We don't have money for repairs; we don't have money for repairs. . . .

I blamed Universal Spirit. "Why aren't you providing for me? I'm trying so hard and learning so much, yet the universe doesn't bring me what I need! I want to trust that you'll always provide; I want to be in flow no matter what happens, but I'm so far from it."

At bedtime, I listened to a meditation with the vibration of abundance, hoping to restore my mind to knowing I always have all I need. But afterward, I couldn't sleep; the new mediation was making changes in me, and my protective mind still wanted to use the old patterns that had always worked. I breathed deeply up and down my central energy channel until I fell asleep.

Weeks later, I stopped at my bank, walking directly to the cashier's desk; conversation flowed easily. Something was different. The bank seemed brighter and warmer. I looked around, seeing the usual wallpaper. I didn't smell fresh paint; the carpet showed a little wear in places.

As I got back in my car, realization hit me. Banks had always seemed cold, dark, and much larger than me. Now I was bigger than the bank! Money brings me things I love—money is the universe sharing its love! My bank account holds dollars plus all the love of the universe; it's bigger than the bank too!

# Chapter 21

# The Biofield of Oneness

One day, I said to Universal Spirit, "What was it like at the beginning of life on earth?"

In a vision, highlights of life experiences flashed into my mind, until I was back in the womb, then to a brief moment before conception, when I was still individuated as me. Then my molecules quickly separated, dispersed, and joined the Oneness as tiny parts of the universe.

Full of wonder and awe, I said, "What was it like when there was only truth?"

Universal Spirit took me in a vision to the unending expanse beyond the biofield of Oneness; I could see and do anything I wanted. Then my molecules gathered until I was in the womb again; a second later, I was in the present time, and the vision was gone.

Wanting to know more about what my spirit remembered

of the universe, I scheduled another hypnosis session. My friend read my questions. "Are stars in the biofield of nature, or are they in the biofield of Oneness with the sun and moon?"

I reached with my senses into the Oneness, surrounded by love and joy. "Stars are in nature, and so are the reflections of the sun and moon we see. The physical sun and moon are in their own biofield within the Oneness. The stars flow in harmony with them."

"Is the energy deep under the earth in the biofield of nature or the Oneness?"

My spirit searched the Oneness. "It has its own biofield within the Oneness, but it also operates within nature. Like the sky clock, it's in both!"

"Are the equinoxes and solstices part of the sky clock?"

Universal Spirit took me in a vision back to when the universe was new. "I made them part of the calendar then."

"What do they symbolize?"

"They show annually what the moon symbolizes monthly— humanity going from abundance to hierarchy and back again."

In a vision the next morning, I was surrounded by a deep sadness emanating from people on earth. Following the light of Universal Spirit through the central channel of the biofield of nature, I emerged at the garden I'd seen before. I assumed the Garden of Eden—or Mount Meru, as some people referred to it—represented this garden. The world was as it had been and will be again—beautiful and joyful.

Universal Spirit said, "All this is in you."

We went higher until the earth spread out beneath me. The moon was below me too, a yellowish- green circle made of light. I stepped into moon energy with all my senses; it felt pleased, happy, and spacious. I did cartwheels back and forth across the circle, even though I had never been able to do a cartwheel on earth.

I said to Universal Spirit, "What causes the phases of the moon? Does a pendulum go back and forth across the moon, like what I saw in my ancient grandfather's drawings?"

Something pressed in on me, flattening me into a slim vertical space. Unable to move, I stayed still and flat. In a moment, the pressure left, and the moon energy and I expanded again. Every flattening was followed by expansion.

Universal Spirit took me into the biofield of the sky clock; four or five suns were spaced evenly in a circle above the biofield of nature. All except one were dark and stationary, but as I watched, they all began spinning and shining, fully restored.

Universal Spirit said, "This will happen."

The following day, my ancient grandfather contacted me from the Oneness. "I want to show you what I know about the sky clock."

During my next hypnosis session, I focused my attention on the outer edge of my ancestral biofield and waited to learn more about my ancient grandfather's life. Soon, I felt his presence in the room.

He said, "I lived a generation after the giant trees were cut down; most people knew the trees had existed but didn't know how important they were. Many changes took place on earth within one hundred twenty years of when the trees were destroyed. I spent much of my life learning about the sky clock and was killed for it."

He continued sharing visions of his life as we traveled through my ancestral field. "I became interested in the giant trees and the sky clock when I was eight years old. Weird things were happening in the weather and sky."

I said, "What did you see?"

"Daylight became dimmer, and the hours of darkness increased."

He continued. "When I was twelve, I learned the trees had recharged the sky clock, nature, and people. After the trees were cut down, the health and mental awareness of most people diminished; they were no longer able to transition to the Oneness when they died."

He said, "When I was seventeen, some people were trying to shut me down; they didn't want me to know about the sky clock."

We were in his midtwenties. "I had to be very careful because I had a family to protect."

At his age of forty-eight, I was in a vision; we were in a cave with an elderly man who had lived while the trees were alive. He handed my ancient grandfather the drawings I had seen in the treasure chest; we left the cave quickly and escaped. The men who had been chasing us killed the old man.

I said, "Can you tell me more of how the sky clock works?"

He paused, trying to find the right words. "After I transitioned, I found that the information I knew when I was alive wasn't accurate; only Universal Spirit knows how it originally worked."

Months later the ancient grandfather came to me during my morning meditation. "I have more knowledge for you when you're ready."

As I leaned into the Oneness during hypnosis again, he took me back into the bottom of the ship; his papers were still in the box. He said, "You couldn't read them before; can you now?"

I spread the papers in front of me; they were full of light. "The words are in spirit!"

I focused on the light while energy flowed into my crown chakra and through my body, storing the knowledge for a later time.

The hypnotist read my next question. "Were the giant trees cut down by humans, by other types of beings, or by machines?"

I felt Ancient Grandfather's response. "It was people in loud machines, who disrupted life."

As severe pain burned my heart, I moaned. "All the pain of the trees and the Oneness is in me, longing to be connected again. And I feel the pain of Universal Spirit yearning for all the parts of the whole!"

My friend said, "Breathe into the pain to heal and release it. Take a deep breath and hold it, let it balance the pain. Now release it."

After a few breaths, the pain subsided. I said, "Can I breathe to take away the pain of Universal Spirit too?"

"Of course."

I took long, deep breaths, holding space for the pain, and healing Universal Spirit. "Ancient Grandfather, there's so much pain! How can I go back to that time, clear the pain, and heal it all?"

"Call on me when you're ready."

# Chapter 22

# My Arrowhead

In a vision with Universal Spirit, I was in an open field of tall grass. The sun was shining bright white with a tint of pale green; the tips of grass swayed in the breeze. I didn't remember this place, and didn't feel I needed to; I realized it wasn't literal.

I dug with my hands; the soil was perfect, and digging was easy. A foot deep, I found a cloth bag covered with dirt. It was filled with silver coins that had no distinct markings; they weren't real either.

As I held the coins, the interpretation came: the sky was the universe; the earth was me. I held the treasure of knowledge and truth within me. Digging—seeking knowledge—was easy. The treasure was the release of my spirit—freedom from all that held me back from fully being me, freedom to follow my spirit's desires.

For several weeks, I had felt the urge to share with others

what I'd learned about life and the waiting place. Is this my spirit's desire?

In a vision, a man came from the east, wearing a light jacket and pants made of heavy cloth. He was miles away, walking steadily over hills and through fields.

Having promised myself to fully express my spirit's desires, no matter what they were, I sat in meditation in the vortex, breathing slowly to help my mind work in harmony. I said to my spirit, "Shall I write a book?"

Joy filled my heart; a smile spread across my face. I wrote every morning following meditation, putting on paper all Universal Spirit shared with my heart.

In a vision months later, the man from the east was bundled against cold wind, lifting his knees high above deep snow. Entering my town, he turned down my street, walked across my yard, and knocked on my door. I held the door open and invited him in; the vision ended.

I continued to write as I learned and worked, taking time to clear as much of my stuck energy and old thought patterns as I could.

The third time I saw the man from the east, he was not a vision. His attention walked through my front yard, into my house, and stood in front of me as I sat in meditation. He said, "Would you like this gift?"

I didn't see a gift, but I held out my hands. His attention went inside me. I felt him looking around, trying to find the best place to leave his gift. Am I safe? Was he going to take something from me? He vibrated with Universal Spirit, so I waited as he placed his gift at the back of my throat chakra and left.

The next day, Universal Spirit took me in a vision into myself to the gift in my throat chakra, then back in time through my life until I was a child in our big farmhouse, then a baby in my mother's womb. I spoke to my baby-self at the moment I had first felt separated from the Oneness. "You always had the Oneness; you were always with the Oneness; you always had all you needed."

A few days later in hypnosis, my friend read my question. "Who is the man who visited you three times? If he's not real, what does he symbolize? What was his gift?"

I felt into the Oneness, wanting only truth. "He traveled to me from the future! He gave me the gift of speaking my truth at all times so that he will hear what he needs to hear."

Weeks later, in a vision, my head turned toward the east. This time a young woman, bundled in a long brown coat with the hood pulled tight, was walking through snow near her home. She was looking for answers; her vibration held anxiety. "Will I know what I need before it's too late?"

Intuition said she lived far away in a northern country, and that I'd meet her one day.

Months later, I said, "Gabriel, I know you and my ancestors in the Oneness are helping me write my book; I want it to touch a million hearts."

Suddenly, someone's attention swirled toward me, when it

was almost touching my face, I felt the vibration of the woman from the northern country. I wasn't sure how to greet her. "Hello, my friend. What do you need?"

She said, "Help us!"

"What do you need?"

"My family is starving . . ."

I could feel her love for Universal Spirit, but my mind reacted from past programming. It's a joke! She wants food for starving children, like in a commercial? Then I felt guilty. What if it's real and she needs food?

At the same moment, she finished her sentence. ". . . for knowledge."

I said, "I want to help you, but I don't know your name or where you live."

I turned to Gabriel. "How can I help her when I don't know who she is!"

Gabriel said, "I'll take care of it."

The woman's energy was dissipating.

"Gabriel, how can I help her? What knowledge does she need? How do I get it to her?"

"Let me do it."

Days later, Universal Spirit took me within, to my throat and the top of my shoulders; I was to speak my truth and share what I have learned. Connecting with my ancestors in the Oneness, I heard my dad. He said, "I'll help you share what you know."

That night, I awakened after a vivid dream; people I knew were experiencing severe trauma. I had seen those friends recently and knew they were safe. As I wondered about the meaning of the dream, a series of recent events flashed through my mind: people online in a group biofield session had seemed scared and scattered in the wind without an anchor; I received an overdraft at the bank because I was too scared about money to check my balance; we had to pay a large fine because I hadn't noticed our car tag had expired a year earlier; advice I'd heard suggesting relationships were the best things to invest in.

I knew Universal Spirit was saying, "It's time. When you began seeking truth, you withdrew from the world to learn. I've nourished you with truth and wisdom; you know who I am and who you are. It's time to share what you've learned."

Still in bed, I placed my hands palms up. "I'm ready."

Energy wooshed into my crown; I squirmed from head to toe. I didn't know what the download was, but I knew it would be revealed. A partial Bible verse came to mind. "For now we see through a glass darkly, then face to face. . . ."

My glasses had broken at bedtime. Again Universal Spirit was saying, "Now is the time; no more dark glasses."

It was time for me to share what my spiritual eyes had learned. "How do I finish and publish the book? How can I share more with others after the book is done? What are my spirit's desires, and how do I fulfill them?"

"You don't need to know the whole path, just the next step."

My most urgent spirit's desire was freedom from my old

thought patterns. To do this, I needed to find the arrowhead my dad had spoken about—my deepest pain.

I received a biofield session to clear more of my blame and unworthy feelings—the mindset of lack. Two days later, I awoke during the night as blame and shame were clearing from muscles and tissues in my left shoulder. The lump where my body stored stress was caused by holding on to blame and shame! I focused on twinges in the left side of my throat and shoulder until each pocket of energy released and flowed out my crown. Blaming myself and others was speaking lies! All things are made of Universal Spirit, so all things are good. If all things are good, there is no offense, so there is no blame. I am free!

My deepest pain had been in the womb; feeling I was unwanted and separated from the Oneness, I'd feared rejection and blamed myself. At that moment in the womb, all I had wanted was to be back in the Oneness where everything was love. But this pain had brought my greatest joy—all my life I had an intense yearning to know and be one with Universal Spirit!

And my next deepest pain—the unworthiness and shame from my three-year-old trauma—had also brought great joy; it allowed me to realize now just how much Universal Spirit valued me!

Dad had said, "You'll find your arrowhead—your deepest pain—and you'll rejoice."

I had thought life was hard, that many situations, thoughts, and fears I'd experienced were bad. I had never felt I was good enough, or did enough, or had enough—spiritually, emotionally, or physically.

But all things were made of Universal Spirit; I had everything I needed within me—there was no lack. Like the tree had said, all was good. Receiving everything in life as good was the mindset of abundance!

Placing my hands on a tree, I broadcast my intention through the universe. "All things in the universe are receiving all things as good."

When the intention was completed, I said, "Thank you, tree, for holding my intention."

Energy surged back to me. "Anything, always. We love you."

Joy filled me. "I love you too."

A biofield practitioner worked six time zones ahead of me to help me receive all things as good. I awoke in the midst of a dream. I had walked into the music room at my old high school; only one other person was in the room—a girl who had often made fun of me. I turned to face her without fear or lack. "I receive all things as good."

I felt a release; energy raced up and down between the back of my head and the back of my thighs. I woke my husband, "Please run the massager on me right now."

I lay face down on the massage bed. "Set the massager on high."

I placed my hand where my thighs met my bottom. "Put it here."

Loud moans and sobs poured out of me until emotion cleared at the root chakra.

"Ok, sacral."

More sobbing; my throat was already hoarse. The vibration of the massager and my cries cleared my solar plexus, heart, high heart, and throat chakras until there was nothing left to release.

Later, the practitioner told me about my session. "I cleared at the right side of your root chakra; it felt as if your dad was holding on to you, not letting shame and blame be released."

I said, "Dad's in the Oneness. The Oneness is joy, love, and abundance; he wouldn't be holding me with blame and shame. But his stuck energy in me could be holding on."

A few days later, I gave myself a session to help me receive all things as good; I included all of my ancestors in the hologram even though many were in the Oneness. I worked an hour in the formative years of gestation through age eight. The mindset of lack had caused us to live with these same patterns for millennia; each generation inherited it from others and added more of their own. Many more ancestors transitioned, all from my father's side.

# Chapter 23

# Getting Closer

In a vision, I traveled to the edge of a cold space with no light; it was full of ancestors. Universal Spirit said, "Ancestors in the waiting place choose when to transition; the energy holding them has to let them go when they're ready. Then they choose which vortex to transition from."

In another vision, Universal Spirit took me back to a time when people transitioned from physical life to the Oneness whenever they were ready. As spiritual wisdom and knowledge were lost, people no longer had the voltage they needed to transition while alive, so they transitioned at the moment of death.

During hypnosis, my friend read one of my questions. "Are ancestors in the waiting place negatively charged energy or just low voltage?"

As usual, my mind interpreted their vibration into words.

"Ancestors have very low voltage, much lower than earth-realm angels do."

She read my next questions. "Ancestors always transition as individuals, but sometimes it feels like they have agreed to come together. Do ancestors in the waiting place communicate with each other? Do they try to help each other?"

The answer came quickly. "They don't help each other. And they can't communicate with each other until they are close to being ready to join the Oneness. As their intention to transition becomes stronger and their spiritual wisdom grows greater, their voltage increases and they become able to communicate with each other."

"Do Gabriels help ancestors transition? Do they help ancestors learn what they need to know about the Oneness and the universe?"

"The waiting place is within the biofield of nature. All the wisdom and knowledge the ancestors need is available to them in the light waves of the universe. When they have the desire and intention to join the Oneness, Gabriels make sure they get there."

As I was giving a biofield session, I said to the seven-year-old friend, "Are you feeling happy today?"

She shook her head. "My daddy's birthday is this week."

He had died when she was three and had transitioned in an earlier session. Using my tuning forks to pull away any energy that wasn't hers, I found her father's mother there, vibrating with sadness and anger. The grandmother had died a few months before the girl's father.

I said to the grandmother, "Are you ready to transition?"

"No."

"Then you have to leave."

She left, but as the session progressed, she came back. I said again, "Are you ready to transition?"

"No," she said, her façade crumbling. "But I want to be."

The tuning forks were almost at the stream of ancestral energy near the girl's body. I said to the grandmother, "You need to decide if you're ready to transition; this is the last place for your own stuck energy to clear."

"I'm ready."

But while the forks worked in the ancestral flow, she said, "I'm ready to see my son."

"Being ready to transition is not about your desire to see your son. You have to vibrate with a desire for the Oneness or you won't be able to go there."

As I cleared her energy with a different fork, she said, "Yes, I desire the Oneness; I want to know the kind of love that I've never had in my own heart."

My young friend said a prayer, and her grandmother joined the Oneness.

When I first started working with ancestors, they came to sessions with the desire to transition, but were often angry, fearful, suspicious, and questioned me about what I was doing and why. Much like emotions that were stuck in the human biofield, they were stuck between life and the Oneness as a result of the mindset they had when they died. They continued to exist in a low voltage of their same vibration.

But more recently, most ancestors came prepared to transition, as if they had already heard and received the knowledge they needed through the grapevine. They knew what they wanted and how to get there. They were full of love, joy, and gratitude. As they transitioned, they glowed with higher voltage, vibrating with confidence in their choice to be in the Oneness.

One friend had changed his perception of the world and was discouraged by the struggle to make changes in his life that his family did not agree with. As I began a session, I felt ancestral sadness and powerlessness; ancestors from his mother's side poured into the session. Mostly male, they were ancient warriors dressed in battle attire and soldiers in uniform.

Intuition spoke through me. "Following your spirit and changing your beliefs about religion and hierarchical control in the world is a representation of your warrior ancestors."

My friend said, "I often feel like I'm fighting while pursuing the truth."

At the end of his session, many ancestors transitioned; they had a message for him. "In following your spirit, you're doing what our spirits always wanted to do but could not. Thank you."

Two of my friends had ancestors on both sides of a centuries-long family feud; the wife's ancestors were on one side, the husband's on the other. We held the intention to clear any ancestral feudal energy that was interfering in their marriage. Many ancestors were present, waiting respectfully through the session, without anger, hatred, animosity, or other resistance between the feuding clans.

When time to transition, the energy vibrated with gratitude for the release of centuries of strife. An ancestor of the wife, who had led a massacre of over one hundred of the husband's ancestors, said, "If I could live my life over again, I would do it differently."

A few days later, as I received another hypnosis session, the hypnotist read from my list of questions. "An ancestor from your mother's side placed a gift in your hands before he transitioned, but your hands were empty. What was the gift?"

In the Oneness, I smelled incense burning; it was the vibration of the love and joy my ancestor had felt in being able to transition. He had given me the gift of gratitude to enrich my life—the gratitude he felt in knowing that as an ancestor he could make a difference for the living.

# Chapter 24

# Alchemy

As I thanked the universe for the puppy that had recently joined our home unexpectedly, Gabriel said, "It was my idea. I wanted you to have this joy."

But after the puppy barked and cried for five long nights, I wasn't feeling joy. Old patterns were flaring: blame, fear of rejection, feeling not enough.

My husband said, "I think we're supposed to learn something from the puppy."

I was having difficulty accepting the situation as good. "What's that?"

"The universe holds us like we hold the puppy. She's safe, loved, and has everything she needs, but she's scared. She's reacting with her mind."

"She doesn't know all things are for her highest good."

I received an email from a friend. "At night, try tying one end of a string to the puppy and the other end to your hand; she'll feel your movements and know she's not alone."

It worked! Missing her littermates at night, she must have felt what I had felt in the womb and when I was three—alone and separated, wanting to return to the Oneness.

Preparing for holiday travel, I said to my husband, "I've made a lot of progress in clearing blocks and restoring pathways, but being with family members often brings back old patterns of fear of being separated and wanting their approval. I yearn for restoration."

He said, "Universal Spirit tells us to create what we want. Try alchemy; tear down all the components of your relationships with your family and rebuild it based on how you want it to be. Redefine the relationship and who you are, as if you're meeting them for the first time."

"I'm not sure I can."

But early the next morning, not awake but not dreaming either, I watched myself tearing down a brick wall in front of me; my family stood on the other side. When the wall was down, I saw that the foundation was cracked and broken, so I tore it out too, remembering times when Dad had taught me how to lay brick.

He would set up brick and mortar along a wall near where he was working and run a string from corner to corner marking where the brick needed to be. He'd show me how to put cement on a brick and how to place it in the row, then he'd go back to his own wall. In half an hour, he'd check my work, point out problems, tear out all the bricks back to where the problem started, and show me how to do it again.

I took a breath; it was time to rebuild the wall. This time I started with a foundation of truth I didn't know when the first wall was built.

For the new foundation, I used the wisdom represented in my spiritual chakras nine through twelve: I know I am spirit and that my spirit is designed to lead my mind; I consciously choose to live as spirit; I live in harmony with the abundance of the universe and receive all things as good; as part of the Oneness always, I express my spirit's desires for the highest good of all.

The string I used to measure the height of each row was spiritual too, chakra eight: I align my mind to hear my spirit; in every present moment, I have the choice between action or reaction.

With a solid foundation in place, I laid the first row. I based it on the energy of the root chakra: the universe is always acting in my favor; I am safe and have everything I need within me.

The sacral was row two: I create my own life; I value myself and know that Universal Spirit values me even more.

Next was row three, the solar plexus: I claim the power and authority of the universe within me as my own.

I laid the fourth row with love: I am loving myself and others by only sending positive thoughts and allowing each of us to live our lives as we choose.

Throat energy was next: I express my spirit's desires

completely, and I listen to what others say without hearing through my own thoughts of lack.

Third eye was the sixth row: I live in every present moment, not regretting my past or worrying about the future, because all things are good.

My wall needed an extra row: my subconscious patterns are aligned with my spirit.

Then the capstone, the crown: I am made of Universal Spirit; I respect each of my family members because they are Universal Spirit, too.

Then I stepped back to look at my work. The wall was good! It was higher and stronger than before and had a broad foundation. But something was different. It had brick-like arms, and above the arms, the wall resembled a head. It was me!

I said to the Oneness, "Thank you, Dad. I receive myself as good. I receive my family as good. All is made of Universal Spirit; all is good."

Reaching out, I held my mother in a bubble of love; she had loved me with all her heart all my life. I embraced each family member with love. In rebuilding those relationships, I rebuilt myself!

# Chapter 25

# The Oneness

I drove past the cemetery one day, grateful for a continued relationship with Dad even after his death. He was often with me from the Oneness, placing a hand on my shoulder, or sharing his love and wisdom. Sometimes his attention was with me as I meditated, worked in the garden, visited my mother, or spoke with her on the phone. I laughed at my own joke. "Well, I don't have to stop there!"

His attention was with me once again, the same humor in his voice as when alive. "No, you don't!"

Through sessions or meditation, I noticed that each ancestor retained their unique personalities and memories of their physical lives. And though non-transitioned ancestors were sometimes nervous, hesitant to interact, or sometimes antagonistic, ancestors in the Oneness seemed to retain only the positive side of their personalities, and were very willing to share their wisdom with me.

Each biofield still had the record of their lives and their stuck energy within it, yet the ancestors seemed to no longer feel unhelpful thought patterns associated with resistance to emotions and situations.

As stuck energy was released from the biofields of their living descendents, ancestors in the Oneness seemed to feel their own energy clearing; they responded with joy and gratitude, their biofields glowed brighter, and their vibrations were stronger.

Feeling Grandma's sadness within me again, I tuned myself. Grandpa and Grandma and I hugged together; they were as relieved and grateful as I was that more of her sadness was gone.

Months later, I received a biofield session to reset my adrenal system. Working on my left side, the practitioner said, "Is your mom sad?"

I was already feeling the sadness. "No, but Grandma was."

"It feels like we're clearing for Grandma too."

"We are; Grandma was here from the Oneness, standing by my side and holding my hand as the energy cleared. She leaned over and kissed my forehead, then left."

Heavy energy in my ancestral river alerted me as the practitioner tuned the right side adrenals. I said to the universe, "Whose energy is this?"

The ancient grandfather who had held my spirit's intention for me before I was born directed his attention to me from the Oneness. "Mine."

"It feels like you're being tortured!"

"Fifty of us were working together, using intention and attention to help people know the truth the hierarchical leaders were hiding; we were tracked down and killed."

He had resembled Abraham Lincoln after all; he had helped set people free! "Did you feel a strong connection with Universal Spirit all your life?"

"I had faith, but I only chose to deepen my spiritual wisdom when I was in prison. I looked into the future, saw you, and learned to hold your spirit's intention."

One day, in meditation, wanting to share the love, joy, wisdom, and knowledge of my ancestors in the Oneness, I said, "Did any of you have difficulties with family relationships? Did you feel you didn't measure up to their expectations?"

The grandfather who held my spirit intentions said, "Yes."

My ancient grandfather, who loved the giant trees and sky clock, agreed.

Dad said, "I didn't measure up to my family because I wasn't part of their church."

Grandpa felt differently; he had exceeded his family's standards. "But when I got to death and found the waiting place, I had many regrets for missing out on what was really important in life. That's why I want to help you; I want my family to know about it before they die."

"Grandpa, what would you have done differently?"

"I would have let it go, let go of working so hard for what the world thinks is important, and held on to what is real."

At the moment that ancestors transitioned into the Oneness, they gained basic knowledge and wisdom about how the universe works and why it works the way it does. But while in the Oneness, they continued to pursue wisdom and have access to all truth from Universal Spirit.

Many ancestors in the Oneness were full of wonder and curiosity about the universe, always wanting to know more. Sometimes when I have asked a question of my ancestors in the Oneness but didn't sense a response right away, I've gotten the feeling they were busy learning, seeing, and experiencing the universe, and too busy to answer me.

By searching and listening in the Oneness, Grandpa had learned about his ancient grandfather, who had known about the sky clock. When this ancient grandfather got to the Oneness, he learned that most of what he knew on earth was error, and said to me, "When I learn more, I'll share it with you."

When ancestors in the Oneness appeared around me, they were like orbs of light, vibrating with a mix of joy, love, gratitude, wonder, and curiosity. They didn't even have a tiny flicker of the mindset of lack. But I wanted to learn more than my senses could feel, and I wanted to be in that wonderful vibration again.

So in hypnosis, I asked my friend to read the next question from my list. "How many biofields does an ancestor in the Oneness have?"

I had only found one biofield with my tuning forks, but I wanted to be sure, so I listened to the Oneness. "They just have one—the record of their own life. Angels have one biofield also. All of them are free to be wherever they want to be within the biofield of Oneness."

"Are there any levels or divisions of authority in the Oneness?"

I listened to the Oneness again. "No. Guardian angels and archangels have different roles, but all angels and ancestors are of equal value. There is no hierarchy."

"Can you feel the vibration of Universal Spirit separately within the Oneness, or is it all one vibration?"

"I feel different vibrations for each part in the Oneness and the vibration of the whole. The vibration of ancestors seems to have a higher percentage of joy, while Universal Spirit and the angels' vibrations are more of a deeper supportive love."

She read the next question. "What do the angels and ancestors in the Oneness want you to know today?"

The vibration of the Oneness said, "Be all you can be. Try whatever you desire; all your spirit's desires are from Universal Spirit. We are here for you."

One day, after asking Universal Spirit for intuition on planning a project, intuition said, "Ask your ancestors in the Oneness for help."

"Do any of my ancestors have wisdom for my project?"

A female said, "I do."

"Who are you?"

"I'm from your mom's side."

I could tell from her vibration that it was a

great-great-great-grandmother! I didn't feel specific guidance from her as I worked, but the project went smoothly and came together in the best way.

Before I began this work, whether I had known them personally or had just heard stories about them, I had felt like I didn't have much in common with any ancestor further back than my grandparents. But connected with them in the Oneness every day, I felt our common intentions for oneness with Universal Spirit and the desire to know how the universe works. They shared the mindset of abundance with Universal Spirit that I strived for. As I cleared my old patterns, I increased their voltage, and in turn, their love and support increased mine.

In a vision one day, the Oneness was bright and happy as ancestors and angels shared and compared with each other what they had learned. Their joy and love flowed vibrantly to me. "We are always with you. We love you."

As they spoke, my head turned toward the window behind me; angels and ancestors stood around me creating electric flow. My heart opened, and their spirits came as one into my own; we were me!

Before tuning myself one day, I said to the Oneness, "If any of my ancestors would like to release what prevented you from speaking your truth, and help me clear what keeps me from speaking my truth, you are welcome in this session."

My paternal grandparents came from the Oneness to join me.

In another self-tuning session, I held my tuning forks at the edge of the ancestral field on my father's side; energy was ready to clear. I said to those ancestors, "Please release easily all the stuck energy keeping you from loving yourselves and keeping me from loving myself fully."

Love from those in the Oneness filled the field. "We'll help."

In one session, a friend and I were working with intention, voice, and movement, to clear stuck energy in her solar plexus chakra, but the energy wouldn't budge. She said, "I feel I need to do something to help my mother, but my siblings are against it."

Energy suddenly began to shift. I said, "Take back your power!"

Her paternal grandfather came from the Oneness. "I'm here with you."

My friend took a deep breath. "I'm going to take back my power and do what needs to be done! My family's negative energy has no power over me!"

Their anger and powerlessness flowed through my forks as I worked in her ancestral field. Voices pulsated as ancestors flooded into the room. "We're here!"

One of her ancient grandfathers said, "I love you. You have all the power you need. Just trust yourself."

Ancestors and guardian angels in the Oneness were always with me, helping me find wisdom and express my desires. Intentionally tapping into this group was powerful; the entire universe held my spirit's intentions with me.

During meditation, Universal Spirit asked for my attention; we went into my third eye, then to the throat, and stopped at my heart. The sadness was painful. Spirit said, "Release it."

As I dropped this sadness into my solar plexus, the ancient grandfather who had held my spirit's intentions helped me drop all the sadness and unworthiness from gestation. As it cleared, my power increased; I knew my worth and my value. My heart overflowed with gratitude. Ancestors from the Oneness stood near me; I reached my hands to join with theirs. "Thank you for holding me until I could hold a loving presence for myself."

Their energy flowed into my heart. "We are one."

I connected in spirit with the Oneness. "The love is so beautiful here! I wish I never had to leave."

They said, "You never do; we're in you. We love you."

They had always been in me, but I had forgotten I was in them. I had lived my whole life with old thought patterns and stuck energy, forgetting I was spirit. My ancestors had done the same.

Unaware of the power within us and how to focus that power to restore ourselves and the universe, we had been running on low voltage for millennia. And at death, most of my ancestors had gone to the waiting place instead of the Oneness.

# Chapter 26

# Knowledge

As more ancestors transitioned, I noticed patterns. Wanting to understand what I was seeing, I said to Universal Spirit, "How does it feel spiritually to a person at the moment of death? How do they know what's going on? How do they know what they need to know to transition?"

Universal Spirit said, "Ask your ancestors."

I said to Grandpa, "What happened at your death? Why did you go to the waiting place instead of the Oneness?"

Grandpa had been an honest, hardworking person who liked to learn about history and finance, not spiritual things. He said, "I wasn't ready. What I knew about life and the afterlife wasn't true; I didn't know enough to transition. I'm helping you now so my family will know the truth."

"How did you find out about the afterlife?"

"After I was there, I watched and learned."

Grandpa had embraced learning all his life; in the afterlife, he learned he was made of Universal Spirit. The energy of the spiritual chakra fifteen to twenty inches below the feet—knowing we are spirit beings—represented that each ancestor needed to learn how the afterlife works.

But fear of the unknown kept another ancestor from watching and learning about the afterlife. A friend sent me a text. "My mother died early this morning."

As I sent intentions of love and comfort to the friend, her mother's spirit entered my home. It vibrated with fear and panic. "I must find my husband; I need his help! Please help me!"

He had died several years earlier; I assumed he had gone to the waiting place too. "Focus your attention and intention on him; he'll hear and come when he's ready. And if you focus on feeling Universal Spirit in every part of you, you'll feel better."

At her funeral, she urged me to tell her children she was there; she wanted me to relay to them what she wanted to tell them. The ancestor had not been in the waiting place long enough to know it was up to her to let her children know she was present and guide them to someone who could help her transition when she was ready.

For months, I had felt lingering energy from a great-great-grandfather; I had cleared his worry and regret in my biofield, but he had not come to transition.

He had secluded himself in his home until he died; he was

still there. All the knowledge an ancestor needs is available in the light waves, but this grandfather hadn't learned that he could transition if he was ready; he thought he had to stay where he was.

Though I was still sitting in the vortex, my spirit stood outside the window of the room he had died in. "You don't have to stay in the house; you can join the Oneness if you want to. You can follow me to my home and transition if you're ready."

As I left, I sensed him pondering the information; soon he followed me home. "Grandfather, thank you for your life; I've learned from this experience. I love you."

I felt his vibration of hope and love as he ascended in the vortex.

Lack of knowledge had kept another of my ancestors in the waiting place. "I'm scared to join the Oneness; maybe God won't want me."

I said, "We'll all be received by the Oneness. We're all wanted there."

Her uncertainty changed to joy, and I watched her transition.

# Chapter 27

# Desire

As most ancestors came to transition, they knew they were made of Universal Spirit, and they had a heart's desire to be with Universal Spirit.

Their minds were more restful, no longer reacting in the chronic pattern of fight, flight, or freeze that most ancestors brought with them to the waiting place when they died. They had learned to align the hemispheres of their mind so they could always hear their spirit's desire for the Oneness. The desire to hear their spirit was represented by the spiritual chakra fifteen to twenty inches above the crown—recognizing that in every present moment they could either react with their mind or listen to their spirit.

Many ancestors who came to transition felt the magnetism of all the parts for the whole. They said, "I so much want to join the Oneness."

At the end of one friend's first ancestral clearing, the ancestor said, "I'm tired of being stuck here. I've been waiting to go to the light."

A man I'd known well during his life came to transition; I could feel his deep desire for Universal Spirit.

I was tuning his young granddaughter, but I didn't want his son to miss this connection with his father. "Your son should be here to acknowledge your transition."

"My son isn't getting around to it; I want to join the Oneness."

I still hesitated.

His voice took on an edge; he knew the rules of the afterlife and had made his choice. "It's my granddaughter, isn't it?"

"Yes."

"Then I can transition."

I was wrong to keep him from his desire; if the son wanted to, he could have a much richer connection when his father was in the Oneness. "You deserve it for all the heartache you had in your life."

He left quickly in the vortex, but in a second, his attention came from the Oneness; he wanted to share his joy with me, knowing I desired Universal Spirit too. "This is all I've ever searched for. It's all I've ever wanted."

I whispered through tears, "I know."

The ancestors who had learned to feel their spirit's yearning for Universal Spirit responded from love instead of reacting to protect themselves or gain advantage over others. They expressed sadness or regret for causing others harm or difficulty.

In one pocket of his life record, I felt an ancestor's uncontrollable rage and the action he had taken to express it. After energy cleared, he expressed his new mindset as spirit, calmly and with regret, but knowing everything worked for good. "What I did was wrong."

One friend and his ancestors shared a desire for the Oneness; their joint intention was felt strongly throughout the light waves; two hundred thirty-two came to transition.

But beside this heart's desire, he and his ancestors shared the same stuck energy pattern: worry. My friend had inherited it from his mother. As I worked to clear worry in the ancestral field, an ancestor from many generations back stepped forward.

He said, "I'm the one who started the pattern; I'm so sorry to have caused this problem for all my family."

My friend said, "It's all right. You didn't know."

# Chapter 28

# Conscious Choice

Another pattern I noticed was that most ancestors who came to transition had already made their choice; they were responding to their spirit's desire—the magnetism of all the parts for the whole. They had embraced the energy of the spiritual chakra three to four feet above the crown—consciously choosing to live as spirit—and they were ready to go home.

Their mindset had already begun to change; fear of lack and the control of hierarchy had begun being restored to the love and abundance of Universal Spirit. Their voltage was higher than the grayscale ancestors who had not yet chosen to transition.

But a few ancestors came to sessions who had not consciously chosen to transition; they expressed anger or unpleasant attitudes, and resisted energy being cleared. They were not attracted to the positive energy of the vortex and left quickly when I told them to.

One day, intuition guided me to the grave of a young man. He was waiting for me. "What are you doing in your home?"

"I help people transition to the Oneness."

"I'm not ready," he said quickly, then paused. "My mom needs me."

"Whenever you're ready, tell your mom to contact me."

I continued walking through the cemetery, but soon his presence was near. "Can my dad help me?"

"Yes."

"What about my brother?"

"Yes."

"Okay, but I'm not ready."

A few months later, I walked by the cemetery again. He said, "I need you to contact my mom for me."

I felt manipulation; he knew that if the living didn't know how to help him, it was his job to communicate with them. He had not chosen to join the Oneness, and he wasn't ready to do everything he could to be there.

# Chapter 29

# Stuck Energy

Although many ancestors had already learned what they needed to know about the afterlife, desired the Oneness, and made their choice to go home by the time they came to transition, there were two more things most of them needed to transition, and both required the help of a living descendent.

Most of the ancestors back to the great- or great-great-grandparents of my friends needed some of their stuck energy cleared before they were able to transition. Sometimes generations further back needed stuck energy cleared also, but often their old patterns and energy were released when the energy of closer relatives was cleared. The closer the generation of an ancestor to a descendent, the higher the percentage of DNA and stuck energy of that ancestor within them.

Just like the giving and receiving of information each person shared with the universe—which was represented in the spiritual chakra just inside the outer edge of the biofield—all the energy shared among generations was good too. Our emotions were important information to help us respond to situations. But resisting those feelings—forgetting the universe always worked in our favor and we always had everything we needed—had resulted in stuck pockets and unhelpful thought patterns in our ancestors and in us.

Usually the energy that needed to be cleared was from a significant time in the ancestor's life, such as mental or physical trauma, the death of a child, or a lifelong pattern of worry—times when the ancestor had much resistance to whatever they were feeling or experiencing.

Often, the stuck energy ancestors needed to be released was formed from what the ancestors were thinking or feeling at their death, such as sadness or regret. One ancestor pushed me off balance, wanting me to clear the worry and regret he felt before he died. When it was cleared, he was ready to transition.

A few ancestors have said, "My life was very difficult; death was a blessing."

As one session ended, many ancestors were ready to transition. "We carried this emotional weight all our lives, and our descendents carried it too. We're glad to be free."

After having energy cleared, another ancestor said, "I feel the freedom I've always wanted to feel."

Some ancestors released their energy to help the living. In one session, the tuning forks were stuck in a deep pocket. I said to the ancestor present, "Please help us clear this."

He said, "I'm here because I wanted to help. I represent generations of ancestors with the mindset of lack who are still waiting to be ready."

As a friend cleared her old thought patterns, her ancestor said, "I came because I wanted to help her; I feel sad she had to go through what she did in her life."

When ancestors came to a session antagonistic or untrusting, their energy was unable to clear; often, it was because they needed to feel their presence was welcomed and they were safe.

If a friend had not been able to feel love toward an ancestor because their relationship had been difficult, then compassion or willingness to help was received as love by the ancestor, and energy was released, bringing healing to both.

In one session, I stood at the edge of the ancestral field; after welcoming my friend's ancestor into the room, I said, "Who are you?"

"A sister."

She paced the room. "I'm not sure I want to stay."

My forks found pockets of the ancestor's stuck energy at birth, in her twenties, and again at death. I said to my friend, "Did you or any ancestor on your mother's side have a sister who died without having children of her own?"

"My great-grandfather. His sister's name was Elizabeth; she was rather cold emotionally, but she was a mother-figure to my mom."

Ancestral energy cleared, but intuition told me to also clear my friend's mother's energy at the time of her conception and gestation. Dense energy wouldn't clear; the mother's stuck emotion wasn't allowing Elizabeth to transition.

I said to my friend, "Send love and compassion to your aunt and your mother; this energy is about the relationship between them—how your mother feels about her."

The stuck energy cleared, but another large pocket presented; my friend had been in her mother's womb when the aunt died; the emotions of the aunt that had affected the mother had influenced my friend.

I said, "Now send love to yourself."

Elizabeth transitioned.

One day, as I was tuning myself, two ancestors stood in front of me. I worked several moments clearing intense emotions in my ancestral field, but even sending love to the ancestors didn't release the energy.

Suddenly, I knew what they had experienced at the moment the energy stuck; they had lived millennia ago when the giant trees were cut down. They had known the spiritual benefits of the trees. I was certain that in earlier sessions I had cleared many layers of their stuck energy caused at the same time. Wanting to acknowledge their pain, I said, "Why couldn't you transition when I cleared your energy before?"

"Our anger was so deep that many layers had to be removed before we could transition."

They were ready now, but they needed one more thing before they could leave in the vortex.

# Chapter 30

# Love

In all my ancestral sessions, the ancestors needed to increase their voltage to be able to make the transition from nature into the biofield of Oneness.

Knowledge is power; once they learned what they needed to know about the afterlife, their voltage increased. Their journey of hearing their spirit's desire for the Oneness, making their choice, and clearing stuck energy all increased their voltage too. But it still took the help of a living person to transition into the Oneness.

The first four generations—parents, grandparents, great-grandparents, great-greats, and often further generations—needed love from a direct descendant to transition. During sessions, this love was often expressed as words. But sometimes it was expressed as the intention to help the ancestor, or by knowing the names of their ancestors and something about their lives. At other times, love was expressed by sending the ancestor on their journey with a sincere blessing.

Although often only ancestors through the fourth generations needed their stuck energy cleared, all ancestors have needed the energy of love, gratitude, appreciation, or compassion from someone living. This was represented in the energy of the spiritual chakra on the outside of the edge of the biofield—knowing we came from the Oneness, will return to the Oneness, and are always part of the Oneness. We are one.

A friend contacted me. "I've received biofield sessions in the past and really felt connected with my ancestors, but recently I've felt a physical block on my right side, between my body and my ancestors. I would really like to clear it."

A great-great-grandfather on his father's side of the family came to his session. "I'm the block. I wanted to go to the Oneness, so I made sure he would do something about it."

As I worked to clear a pocket of ancestral energy, I said to the friend, "Your ancestor worried a lot about his children when he was thirty to thirty-five years old."

"When my great-great-grandfather was in the civil war, he had three young children at home. Soldiers from the opposing side came to his house and took the horses and livestock; his parents hid the children in a cave so they were safe."

The grandfather said, "Thank you for remembering my life."

After at least one ancestor within the first four generations of a family transitioned, ancestors of generations further back were often able to transition without the direct attention from a descendent, but still needed the voltage from a living person.

While walking one day, I held the intention to help ancestors beyond the third and fourth generations from families who already had started ancestral clearing with me. Ancestors gathered all around and followed me home; sixty-seven transitioned, then one more—a young child, whom I took by the hand and walked to the vortex, assuring her that all was good.

Ancestors who didn't have children of their own sensed the intentions of friends or relatives to know which person would be most likely to help them transition and contacted them.

In one session, a friend said, "The past few weeks, I've had frequent memories of a close friend who died in an accident when we were in college twenty years ago. I saw the accident happen."

Just then, a cool breeze swept the room; an ancestor was present. The tuning forks hit a dense pocket in my friend's ancestral field; it was energy that had become stuck at the ancestor's death.

Car tires squealed; people were running to help her. "What's the name of your friend?"

"Susan."

I turned toward the ancestor. "Are you Susan?"

I felt her gratitude for being acknowledged. "Yes."

After several moments, the energy still hadn't released. I said to my friend, "Please send this ancestor your love."

As my friend spoke with love and gratitude for their close friendship, energy cleared and the ancestor transitioned.

Another friend had been feeling the presence of a former boyfriend who had died several years earlier. "I loved him very much, but our relationship was emotionally toxic; I want to release it from my life, and I want to help him transition if he's ready."

The ancestor entered the room as I pulled away thick spiritual resistance from my friend and her ancestral field. Intuition prompted me; I said to my friend, "Call your guardian angel to help you. We need to protect your spiritual rights."

Then I turned to the ancestor. "Call your guardian angel too."

Speaking to both of them, I said, "Now claim your spiritual rights as I name them."

I spoke aloud the spiritual rights every sentient being has, they repeated them, and the energy cleared. Later I said to my friend, "Energy is stuck in your throat chakra; tell your ancestor everything you need to say."

She poured out her heart. Before leaving in the vortex, her ancestor said to her, "Good job! I love you too."

All ancestors who have come to transition always wait for my permission before using the vortex. If they didn't need a descendant's energy to transition, they needed mine because I held the intention to help them.

But they also waited for my permission because it's the mindset of Universal Spirit; it was their free choice to use the vortex in my home. But it was also my free choice to allow the one in my home to be used.

Grandpa and several more of my ancestors had transitioned before I knew a vortex was in my living room. I said to Universal Spirit, "What vortex did Grandpa use?"

For a second, I saw the location: a wooded area on his farm.

Following a car accident, my dad had been in a drug-induced coma for three weeks before he died. At death, he went directly to the Oneness. In meditation, I said to him, "Where did you transition?"

He didn't know. But he knew the answer to my next question.

# Chapter 31

# The Living

The five things that ancestors needed to leave our realm and join the Oneness were their spirit's primary desires, represented in each of the five spiritual chakras. Ancestors needed to learn they were spirit and how the afterlife works. They had to hear their spirits' desires for the Oneness, desire Oneness with all their hearts, and consciously chose to transition. When they were ready, ancestors needed help to release their stuck energy and provide enough voltage to transition. And finally, they needed their descendents to help them.

But what did the living need to transition? What do I need?

I said, "Dad, I know you didn't go to the waiting place when your body died; you transitioned into the Oneness. What happened at the moment of death?"

He said, "I could see all of you around me in the hospital room; I wanted to talk to you, but I couldn't."

"I wish I would have known then how to connect with you by spirit! How were you able to transition into the Oneness?"

"My Gabriel told me what I needed to know, and I chose to go to the Oneness."

I knew that, for most of his life, he had the heart's desire for Universal Spirit; that was all he needed at death, except to make his choice to go! Gabriel had provided all the rest, including taking him to the vortex nearest the hospital.

I told my husband what I'd learned from Dad. "I'm thankful to know about what happens at death, but now I'd like to know how people can transition while they're still living, which I saw in a vision could be done millennia ago."

He said, "We learn to live by our minds, not our spirits, even though we're spirit beings. We have lots of negative thought patterns and stuck energy, yet everyone eventually goes to the Oneness. So why are we here? What's the purpose of our physical existence?"

"I think we're here so we can choose to return to the Oneness by our own free will."

But I wanted to know for sure, so I asked the hypnotist to read my questions. "During one of your first hypnosis sessions, you discovered that you were in the Oneness before you were born. Universal Spirit had a purpose or project for you, so you chose to live in a physical body. What was the purpose or project you came for?"

As my senses felt into the Oneness, the answer wasn't what I expected. "We come to earth to know we're made of Universal

Spirit and to create the world by being all our spirits desire to be! We're not just allowed to create our life; the full expression of our spirits' desires is mandatory for the universe to be all it can be!"

Even though our old emotional patterns caused roadblocks within us, and though the universe carried sadness for not having the vital daily connection with each of us it was meant to have, all we needed to fulfill our purpose was within us!

During my friend's first session, as I grounded his energy to Universal Spirit deep under the earth, his heart's desire to know the love and truth of Universal Spirit flowed through the forks, bringing tears to my eyes.

Universal Spirit said, "He hears my call."

After relaying the message to my friend, I said, "Love is the magnetism of the whole yearning for all the parts; your heart's desire is the magnetism of the parts for the whole."

As his ancestors transitioned, he said, "What's God's call for my life?"

"It's the same as His call to all of us: He wants us to know who we are as an integral part of Him, and to create our lives by fully expressing our individual spirit's desires for the highest good of all. I think knowledge of the afterlife was purposefully hidden through the centuries because if we knew we were spirit, we'd have the power to change ourselves and the world."

Like many of the ancestors in the waiting place, I had waited, powerless, most of my life, because I didn't know who I was. Thinking I lacked—that I was unworthy and not enough—I'd held on to fear instead of remembering I was always safe. Clearing the old patterns within me and my ancestors helped open me to the abundance of love, gratitude, and joy of the universe.

In a vision, Universal Spirit took me to a time when every being who ever existed was in the Oneness again; all the energy of the universe was Oneness. Everyone was in the present moment; whatever we wanted to see or experience was brought into reality in front of us; when our thoughts changed, the energy melded and made new. I said to the ancestors in the Oneness, "Are you looking forward to this?"

I felt their joy and love of knowing that not only did they have the abundance of Universal Spirit now within the biofield of Oneness, but that all of the universe would be Oneness again forever.

As I hugged a tree in front of my home, hands on its bark and bare feet on soil, the tree said, "What intention are you holding today?"

I sent the intention to transmute all the harmful frequencies into helpful ones. And I held the intention to restore my heart and mind.

Tree said, "Hold me."

Why did it say that? I'm already holding it.

I went inside for meditation, sat in my grandmother's rocker in the center of the ley line vortex, and sent my love radiating through the universe.

Universal Spirit said, "Hold me."

Then I knew. As I hugged the tree again, I pictured in my mind the Oneness as I had seen in a vision, when all who ever existed were standing as one, and held their joy and love in my heart. Then, holding Universal Spirit's intention on behalf of every part and the whole, I said, "I am holding all people living and all generations yet to live, all ancestors and angels in the waiting place, all of nature, and all of the Oneness, including the sky clock and the deep energy. I hold you, Universal Spirit."

As all parts of the universe stood with me and spoke as one, the river of love I usually felt from my ancestors became an ocean. "We know we are spirit, we align our minds to hear our spirit, we choose to live as spirit, we are living in harmony with the abundance of the universe and receiving everything as good, and we are fully expressing ourselves for the highest good of all, for our own restoration, and for the restoration of all things."

As my spirit's intention was broadcast through the trees, the energy of the universe expanded into all it was meant to be—full capacity unknown since the beginning—amplified limitlessly beyond the biofield of Oneness into unending Universal Spirit, then came back to me. We were one. The power I needed to fully be all my spirit can be and for the restoration of all things was always within me.

"I give thanks. And so it is."

And with gratitude for the many people whose expressions of their spirits' desires encouraged me to express my own, I have listed names and links in Resources to help others on their journeys.

Also included in Resources are links to a free biofield session, *Clearing Your Future, Clearing Your Past*, and illustrations of a few of the ideas presented in this book.

# Resources

Please visit the Ancestral River website to download the free recorded biofield session, "Clearing Your Future, Clearing Your Past" at https://www.ancestralriver.com/free-session or by using this QR code:

Links to the resources below, as well as to illustrations of the four biofields, the spiritual chakras, and the energy protection meditation, can be found at https://www.ancestralriver.com/resources or by using this QR code:

Resources are listed in the order they became part of my. I benefited from free webinar presentations offered through email communications and free YouTube channel videos, as well as through books and paid courses. On the website, click on each name, and you can read how I benefited from each. As my journey continues, more helpful links that I experience in the future will be added on the website.

The resources marked * are affiliate links to digital recordings that I have used personally and benefitted from in my journey. I receive a compensation for each purchase at no additional cost to you.

Crrow777 Radio: Website

Dr. Claire Zammit: Feminine Power

Eileen Day McKusick: Biofield Tuning, "Tuning the Human Biofield" and "Electric Body, Electric Health"

Marci Shimoff, Dr. Sue Morter, and Lisa Garr: Your Year of Miracles

Dr. Sue Morter: The Energy Codes and "The Energy Codes"

Dr. Joe Dispenza: YouTube

Lynne McTaggart: YouTube

Marie Diamond: Website

Anthony Robert and Angela Carter: BioEnergyCode*

Ken Honda: "Happy Money"

William Walker Atkinson: "Thought Vibration"

Grow Your Own Vegetables: Spirit Gardening course

Donna Eden: Eden Energy Method, Website and YouTube

Amara Strand: YouTube

Mandy Morris: website and "The 8 Secrets to Powerful Manifesting"

Oliver Nino: Website and "The Spiritual Activator"

Archaix: YouTube

Kim E. Woods: Website and "All About Magic, beginnings"

Rob Williams: Psych-K

Mary Lee: Manifestation 3.0 and Money Magnet*

Jackie Jones: 7 Magic Experiments*

Alexander Wilson: Manifestation Magic*

Rina Bogart: Mystery School Code*

Dr. Steve G. Jones: Total Money Magnetism*

Image used under license from Shutterstock.com

# Author Biography

Carla Adams had experienced a variety of careers and skills, but after an unexpected change in her life, she discovered her spiritual gifts of feeling the presence of her ancestors and communicating with them. She found that her life-long feelings of sadness, fear, and unworthiness had been the patterns of her ancestors for many generations. By using tuning forks in her biofield and meditating daily, the old patterns shifted. Soon she began helping others through ancestral clearing. Adams lives in the rural Midwest and continues her spiritual journey.